DK EYEWITNESS TOP 10 TRAVEL GUIDES

MILAN
AND THE LAKES

REID BRAMBLETT

Left **Villa Balbianello, Lake Como** Centre **Stazione Centrale, Milan** Right **Isola Bella: Borromeo Tombs**

LONDON, NEW YORK,
MELBOURNE, MUNICH AND DELHI
www.dk.com

Produced by Blue Island Publishing

Reproduced by Colourscan, Singapore
Printed and bound in China by
Leo Paper Products Ltd

First published in Great Britain in 2003
by Dorling Kindersley Limited
80 Strand, London WC2R 0RL
A Penguin Company

**Copyright 2003, 2007 © Dorling
Kindersley Limited, London**

Reprinted with revisions 2005, 2007

A CIP catalogue record is available from
the British Library.

ISBN 13: 978-1-4053-1698-9

Within each Top 10 list in this book, no
hierarchy of quality or popularity is
implied. All 10 are, in the editor's
opinion, of roughly equal merit.

Contents

Milan and the Lakes Top 10

Highlights of Milan
and the Lakes   6

Leonardo's Last Supper,
Milan   8

Milan's Duomo   10

Pinacoteca di Brera, Milan   12

Castello Sforzesco, Milan   16

Pinacoteca Ambrosiana,
Milan   18

Sant'Ambrogio, Milan   20

Lake Maggiore's Isole
Borromee   22

Certosa di Pavia   24

Bergamo   26

Mantova   28

Moments in History   32

Lombard Experiences   34

Notable Milanese
Buildings   36

Left **Lake Lugano vineyards** Centre **Rocca di Angera, Lake Maggiore** Right **Gelato shop**

Churches	38
Museums	40
Lakeside Attractions	42
Villas and Gardens	44
Small Towns and Villages	46
Artists Working in Lombardy	48
Books and Films set in Lombardy	50
Festivals and Events	52
Shopping Meccas in Milan	56
Things to Buy	58
Entertainment Venues in Milan	60
Attractions for Children	62
Cafés and Wine Bars	64

Culinary Highlights of Lombardy	66
Restaurants	68

Around Milan and the Lakes

Milan's Historic Centre	72
Northern Milan	84
Southern Milan	92
Lake Maggiore	98
Lake Como	106
Lake Garda	116
Smaller Lakes and Towns	124

Streetsmart

Practical Information	132
Places to Stay	144
Index	150

Left **Galleria Vittorio Emanuele II, Milan** Right **Mantova**

 Key to abbreviations
Adm *admission charge payable* **A/C** *air conditioning*

3

TOP 10 OF MILAN AND THE LAKES

Leonardo's Last Supper
8–9

Milan's Duomo
10–11

Pinacoteca di Brera
12–15

Castello Sforzesco
16–17

Pinacoteca Ambrosiana
18–19

Sant'Ambrogio
20–21

Lake Maggiore's Isole Borromee
22–23

Certosa de Pavia
24–25

Bergamo
26–27

Mantova
28–29

Top 10 of Everything
32–69

MILAN AND THE LAKES

TOP 10 Highlights of Milan and the Lakes

Milan is Italy's economic powerhouse, a bustling city of finance and industry, media empires and fashion houses, backed up by an impressive cultural heritage of important art galleries and ancient churches. Yet a 40-minute train ride takes you to the azure pools of "the lakes", lined with fishing villages, villas and laid-back resorts.

Lake Como

1 Leonardo's Last Supper
One of the largest and most ingenious works created by the ultimate Renaissance Man. It is in an advanced state of deterioration now, but even the shadow that remains of this great work can teach us volumes about Renaissance ideals *(see pp8–9)*.

2 Milan's Duomo
The world's largest Gothic cathedral took more than 400 years to complete, a forest of stone pinnacles, flying buttresses, more than 3,500 statues and fantastic panoramas from its roof *(see pp10–11)*.

3 Pinacoteca di Brera
Northern Italy's greatest painting gallery displays masterpieces by Mantegna, Giovanni Bellini, Piero della Francesca, Raphael and Caravaggio *(see pp12–15)*.

400 yards 0 metres 400

4 Castello Sforzesco
A sprawling 15th-century castle, now home to collections of tapestries, archaeological artifacts, paintings by Bellini and Mantegna, and sculptures that include Michelangelo's final work, the *Rondanini Pietà (see pp16–17)*.

Previous pages **Milan's Gothic Duomo**

Pinacoteca Ambrosiana 5

This cultural study centre founded in the 17th century contains works by Leonardo, Botticelli, Raphael and Caravaggio *(see pp18–19)*.

The Lakes map labels:
Colico, Sondrio, Alpi Orobie, Lago Maggiore, Lago di Como, Val Camonica, Isole Borromee 7, Varese, Lago di Lecco, Lecco, Bergamo 9, Lago d'iseo, Lago di Garda, Busto Arsizio, Monza, Brescia, Rho, MILAN, Sesto S. Giovanni, Lonato, Novara, Vigevano, Crema, Crema, Mortara, Certosa di Pavia 8, Lodi, Cremona, Mantova 10, Pavia, miles / km 40

Sant'Ambrogio 6

One of the oldest churches in Milan, it was founded by the city's bishop and patron saint Ambrose in 379. It's filled with mosaics and carvings dating back to the 4th century *(see pp20–21)*.

Lake Maggiore's Isole Borromee 7

Three verdant islands, one still dominated by a fishing village, the other two clad in the sumptuous villas and ornate gardens of the local ruling Borromeo clan *(see pp22–3)*.

Certosa di Pavia 8

The pinnacle of the Lombard Renaissance, a vast monastery and church complex in the Po plains with an ornate marble façade, exquisite carved tombs, and some excellent paintings and frescoes *(see pp24–5)*.

Bergamo 9

The perfect balance of small town charm and sophisticated culture, medieval streets and Renaissance buildings, chic boutiques and hearty home-cooking *(pp26–7)*.

Mantova 10

The ancient seat of the Gonzaga dukes – ringed on three sides by shallow lakes – boasts Renaissance palaces designed and decorated by the likes of Mantegna and Giulio Romano *(see pp28–9)*.

🔟 Leonardo's Last Supper

The Last Supper, *Leonardo da Vinci's 1495–7 masterpiece, is a touchstone of Renaissance painting. Since the day it was finished, art students have journeyed to Milan to view the work, which takes up a refectory wall in a Dominican convent next to the church of Santa Maria delle Grazie. The 20th-century writer Aldous Huxley called it "the saddest work of art in the world": he was referring not to the impact of the scene – the moment when Christ tells his disciples "one of you will betray me" – but to the fresco's state of deterioration.*

Santa Maria delle Grazie

🕐 Book as far ahead as possible, especially if you are visiting during the holidays.

The informative audio guide will help explain why such a deteriorated fresco is nevertheless so important.

🍴 A few blocks down Via Magenta at via Carducci 13, Bar Magenta takes up a wide corner, a pleasing blend of Art Nouveau café and Guinness pub *(see p65).*

• Map J3 • Tourist info: Piazza S Maria delle Grazie 2/Corso Magenta, Milan • 02-8942-1146
• www.cenacolovinciano.it
• 8:15am–6:45pm Tue–Sun • €6.50 plus €1.50 booking fee; free for EU citizens under 18 or over 65

Top 10 Features

1. Groupings
2. "Halo" of Jesus
3. Judas
4. The Table
5. Perspective
6. Light
7. Reflections
8. Coats of Arms Above Painting
9. Crucifixion on Opposite Wall
10. Example of Ageing

1 Groupings

Leonardo was at the time studying the effects of sound and physical waves. The groups of figures reflect the triangular Trinity concept (with Jesus at the centre) as well as the effect of a metaphysical shock wave, emanating out from Jesus and reflecting back from the walls as he reveals there is a traitor in their midst.

2 "Halo" of Jesus

The medieval taste for halos is satisfied without sacrificing Renaissance realism: Christ is set in front of a window *(below)*, giving him the requisite nimbus without looking as if he's wearing a plate for a hat.

3 Judas

Previously Judas was often painted across the table from everyone else. Leonardo's approach is more subtle, and instead he places the traitor right among the other disciples *(above)*.

4 The Table

The table probably uses the same cloth and settings that the monks would have used, heightening the illusion that they were sharing their meals with Jesus and the Apostles.

For more on Leonardo da Vinci see p48

5 Perspective
The walls of the room in the painting appear to be continuations of the walls of the actual room you are standing in. The lines zoom in on Christ at the centre, drawing your eye towards his and helping to heighten the drama.

6 Light
Note the brilliant effects of the carefully worked interaction between the three sources of light – from the refectory itself, from the windows painted in the background, and from the windows on the refectory's left wall.

7 Reflections
A detail that heightens the illusion of reality: the colours of the disciples' robes are reflected in the glasses and pewter plates on the table (above).

8 Coats of Arms Above Painting
The lunettes (below), which are situated above the fresco, were also painted by Leonardo. It seems that he was as happy painting the perfect leaves around the Sforza coats of arms as he was composing the vast scene below.

9 Crucifixion on Opposite Wall
Most people spend so much time gazing at the Last Supper that they never notice the 1495 fresco by Donato Montorfano on the opposite wall, still rich with colour and vivid detail.

10 Example of Ageing
Montorfano's Crucifixion was painted in true buon fresco, but the now barely visible kneeling figures to the sides were added later on dry plaster – the same method Leonardo used.

A Vanishing Fresco

Rather than paint in buon fresco (the technique of applying pigment to wet plaster so that the colours bind with the base), Leonardo used oil paint on semi-dry plaster. Unfortunately, the image began to deteriorate even before he had finished the work.
To worsen matters, Napoleon's troops used the fresco for target practice, and bombs during World War II ripped off the building's roof. A recent restoration removed centuries of over-painting by early "restorers" and filled in the completely vanished bits with pale washes.

Milan's Duomo

Milan's cathedral took almost 430 years to complete, from its 1386 inception to the façade's finishing touches in 1813 under Napoleon, but the builders stuck tenaciously to the Gothic style. In sheer figures it is impressive: it's the third largest church in the world, it has more than 3,500 exterior statues and is supported by 52 massive columns inside.

View of the roof

🚫 You cannot enter if your shoulders are bare or your shorts or skirt rise above mid-thigh; bring a light shawl or two.

On Milan's rare smog-free days, the view from the roof stretches across the plains as far as the Alps.

🍴 You're spoilt for café choice around here, but nothing beats a Campari at historic Zucca just inside the Galleria Vittorio Emanuele *(see pp64 & 80)*.

• Map M4 • Piazza del Duomo, Milan
• 02-8646-3456
• Cathedral: 7am–7pm daily, free
• Roof: 9am–5.45pm (to 4:15pm 16 Feb–14 Nov) daily, €5 by elevator, €3.50 by stairs
• Museo del Duomo: Piazza del Duomo 14, 10am–1:15pm, 3–6pm daily, €6
• Cumulative ticket for roof and museum €7

Top 10 Highlights

1. Façade
2. Naves
3. Battistero Paleocristiano
4. Stained-Glass Windows
5. Funerary Monument to Gian Giacomo Medici
6. St Bartholomew Flayed
7. Ambulatory and Crypt
8. Ascent to Roof
9. La Madonnina
10. Museo del Duomo

Façade
From the 16th century, various top architects submitted designs for the façade, but it wasn't until 1805–13 that the Neo-Gothic frontage with its bronze doors and reliefs *(above)* was finally built. In 2002, the Duomo's exterior went under scaffolding for a major cleaning set to last a few years.

Naves
The interior *(right)* is a thicket of 52 pilasters ringed with statues of saints in niches. The Gothic "tracery" on the vaulting of the four outer naves is actually ingenious trompe-l'oeil paintings dating from the 16th century. The gloom helps the illusion.

3 Battistero Paleocristiano
A stairway near the entrance leads down to Paleochristian excavations, which have uncovered traces of Roman baths from the 1st century BC, a baptistery from AD 287 and a 4th-century basilica.

The Duomo's façade before cleaning

For more marvellous churches in Lombardy see pp38–9

Stained-Glass Windows

4 Dozens of stained-glass windows *(left)* create splashes of coloured light in the otherwise gloomy interior. The oldest, on the right aisle, date from 1470; the newest from 1988.

Funerary Monument to Gian Giacomo Medici

5 Leone Leoni created the 1560–3 Michelangelesque tomb of a local mercenary general, including a life-sized bronze of the man dressed in Roman centurion armour.

St Bartholomew Flayed

6 Marco d'Agrate's gruesome carving of 1562 shows the unfortunate saint with muscles and veins exposed and his flayed skin thrown rather jauntily over one shoulder.

Ascent to Roof

8 Climb or take the lift up to the roof to explore the cathedral's remarkable Gothic crown of spires, gargoyles, statues and tracery *(above)* – and for the views *(see also p34)*.

La Madonnina

9 Perched at the top of the Duomo's central spire, 108 m (354 ft) above ground level, the gilded copper "Little Madonna" *(right)* has governed over Milan's best panorama since 1774. For centuries she reigned as the highest point in the city until the Pirelli Tower *(see p37)* stole her title.

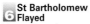
Duomo plan

Ambulatory and Crypt

7 The ambulatory is now open only to worshippers, but you can see a lovely example of a 14th-century Lombard sacristy door. Stairs nearby lead down into the crypt, where the body of Saint Charles Borromeo rests in a crystal coffin, and to the treasury, which is filled with elegant reliquaries and liturgical devices.

La Fabbrica del Duomo

There's no better example of Milanese tenacity than the fact that their cathedral is a totally unspoilt example of the Gothic style, despite taking a full 427 years to build. The generations of builders somehow ignored the siren calls of every new style that came along, from Renaissance, then Baroque, to Neo-Classical. The phrase *la fabbrica del Duomo* – "the building of the Duomo" – in Milanese dialect is still used to refer to anything that seems to take forever to complete.

Museo del Duomo

10 The museum, housed in the neighbouring Palazzo Reale *(see p73)*, contains stained-glass windows and tapestries removed from the Duomo for safekeeping. There is a masterpiece by Tintoretto, *The Infant Christ among the Doctors*, and wooden models of the Duomo.

〇10 Pinacoteca di Brera

Milan's Brera is unique among Italy's major art galleries in that it isn't founded on the riches of the church or a noble family, but the policies of Napoleon, who suppressed churches across the region and took their riches off to galleries and academies. Over the next two centuries, the collections grew to take in some of the best Renaissance-era painting from northern Italy, representatives of the Venetian school and several giants of central Italy, including Raphael and Piero della Francesca.

1 Umberto Boccioni's Riot in the Galleria

In this work of 1911 *(above)*, the Milanese are dashing for the doors of Caffè Zucca *(see p64)*. A companion, *The City Rises*, is also here.

Pinacoteca di Brera

🎧 Make sense of the works on display with the excellent audio guides.

Cheap guided tours for any number of people are available weekdays, but must be booked 2–3 days in advance.

🍷 The bars of the Brera district *(see p90)* make for great snacking or a post-gallery apéritif.

• Map M2 • Via Brera 28, Milan • 02-722-631; information line 02-8942-1146 • www.brera.beniculturali.it • 8:30am–7:15pm Tue–Sun • Adm €5; free for EU citizens under 18 or over 65

Top 10 Works of Art

1. Riot in the Galleria
2. Valle Romita Polyptych
3. Dead Christ
4. Virgin and Child
5. Finding the Body of St Mark
6. Montefeltro Altarpiece
7. Marriage of the Virgin
8. Supper at Emmaus
9. Bacino di San Marco
10. The Kiss

2 Gentile Fabriano's Valle Romita Polyptych

The Brera worked hard to reconstitute this altarpiece of 1410. The five main panels came with Napoleon; the other four were tracked down and purchased later.

3 Mantegna's Dead Christ

Mantegna was one of the Renaissance's greatest perspective virtuosos, and this is his foreshortened masterpiece, painted in about 1500 *(below)*.

Canaletto's Bacino di San Marco

4 Giovanni Bellini's Virgin and Child

The Brera houses several masterpieces by the early Venetian Renaissance master Bellini, including two very different versions of *Virgin and Child*. One is almost a Flemish-style portrait, painted when Bellini was 40. The other is a luminous scene of colour and light, painted 40 years later.

5 Tintoretto's Finding the Body of St Mark

Tintoretto uses his mastery of drama and light in this work of the 1560s to highlight the finding of the body of St Mark by Venetian merchants in the Crusades.

6 Piero della Francesca's Montefeltro Altarpiece

This 1472 scene shows Piero's patron the Duke of Montefeltro kneeling before the Virgin and Child. Just months earlier, the Duke's beloved wife had given birth to a male heir who tragically died within weeks.

Pinacoteca di Brera

Entrance

7 Raphael's Marriage of the Virgin

In this early work depicting the Virgin Mary's terrestrial marriage to Joseph, Raphael took the idea and basic layout from his Umbrian master Perugino, tweaking it with a perfected single-point perspective.

8 Caravaggio's Supper at Emmaus

This 1605 work *(above)* was Caravaggio's second painting of the Supper. The deep black shadows and bright highlights create mood and tension.

9 Canaletto's Bacino di San Marco

The undisputed master of 18th-century Venetian city-scapes did at least seven versions of this scene of St Mark's bell tower and the Doge's Palace *(above)*.

10 Francesco Hayez's The Kiss

This passionate 1859 scene *(left)* – painted when Hayez was 68 – was intended as an allegory of the struggle for independence and the importance of family.

The Palace

The late Baroque Palazzo di Brera was built from 1591 to 1658 as a Jesuit college, but not completed until 1774, after the Jesuits were dissolved. The vast courtyard centres around a bronze statue of Napoleon in the guise of Mars. It was commissioned in 1807, but did not arrive until 1859.

Brera gallery-goers

The Brera Collections

Titian's *Portrait of Count Antonio Porcia*

1 13th-Century Paintings (Rooms II–IV)

Italian art simply wouldn't be the same without the naturalism, bright colours and emotive qualities that Giotto brought to the world of painting, and his influence is clear in works such as *Three Scenes from the Life of St Columna* by Giovanni Baronzio of Rimini. Other works here trace the Gothic style from Central Italy (Ambrogio Lorenzetti and Andrea di Bartolo) to Venice (Lorenzo Veneziano and Jacopo Bellini). The best works are Ambrogio Lorenzetti's *Virgin and Child* and Gentile da Fabriano's *Valle Romita* polyptych.

2 Jesi Collection of 20th-Century Art (Room X)

When Maria Jesi donated her fine hoard in 1976, the

Valle Romita polyptych

Brera became the first major museum in Italy to acquire a significant 20th-century collection. Boccioni's *Riot in the Galleria* is highlighted on p12; other master-works are by Morandi, Severini, Modigliani, Picasso and Braque.

3 Venetian Renaissance (Rooms V-X; XII; XIV)

It is the art of Venice that steals the show at the Brera, and the bulk of the museum's important and memorable works fill these ten rooms: Mantegna's *Dead Christ (see p12)* and numerous superlative works by his brother-in-law Giovanni Bellini. It all culminates in the brushy, stormy, wonderously lit and intriguingly coloured scenes of Venice's High Renaissance trio: Tintoretto, Titian and Paolo Veronese.

4 Lombard Renaissance (Rooms XIII; XV-XIX)

The stars of the Lombard section are the 16th-century Campi clan from Cremona, painters inspired by Raphael and, above all, Leonardo da Vinci. Tiny room XIX is devoted to the direct heirs of the Leonardo revolution: Il Bergognone and Bernardino Luini.

5 Marchese Renaissance (Rooms XXI; XXIII)

These rooms feature Flemish-inspired artists and 15th-century

Raphael's *The Marriage of the Virgin*

painters from the central Marches province. The latter took local art from the post-Giotto Gothicism into a courtly Early Renaissance style, exemplified by Carlo Crivelli.

Tuscan Renaissance (Rooms XXIV–XXVII)

The paintings here are few, but they're stunners: Piero's *Monte-feltro Altarpiece* and Raphael's *Marriage of the Virgin* (both on p13), alongside works by Bramante, Signorelli and Bronzino.

17th-Century Bolognese Renaissance (Room XXVIII)

As Florence and Rome got swept away with Mannerist fantasies and experiments, Bolognese artists held the line on Classical Renaissance ideals. In this room we see Ludovico Caracci, Il Guercino and Guido Reni engaged in an ever more crystalline and reductive naturalistic style.

Caravaggio and his Followers (Room XXIX)

Caravaggio's use of harsh contrast and dramatic tension in paintings such as the *Supper at Emmaus* (p13) influenced a generation of painters. The works of some of the best of them – Mattia Preti,

Jusepe de Ribera and Orazio Gentilleschi – are hung here too.

Baroque and Rococo (Rooms XXX–XXXVI)

In the late 16th century, Italy moved from Renaissance naturalism to the ever more ornate stylings of the Baroque, with Daniele Crespi and Pietro da Cortona to the fore. The Baroque fed off its own overblown conventions until it became Rococo, a style heralded by Tiepolo and Giuseppe Maria Crespi.

19th-Century Painting (Rooms XXXVII–XXXVIII)

There's not so much to pique one's interest in these final rooms, save Francesco Hayez's monumental scenes and the pseudo-Impressionist Macchiaioli school (Fattori, Segantini and Lega).

Modigliani's *Portrait of Moise Kisling*

15

ⓉⓄⓅ10 Castello Sforzesco

This massive, sun-baked rectangular bastion in Milan is actually a complex of fortresses, castles and towers begun in 1451 for Francesco Sforza, largely restored in 1893–1904, and again after massive World War II damage. Its many collections include art and sculpture from the early Middle Ages to the 18th century, decorative arts, musical instruments, Oriental art, and archaeology.

Madonna in Glory by Mantegna

Main gate

Top 10 Highlights

1. Rondanini Pietà
2. Funerary Monument for Gaston de Foix
3. Sala delle Asse
4. Madonna in Glory
5. Madonna and Child
6. Poet Laureate
7. Primavera
8. Trivulzio Tapestries
9. Civico Museo Archeologico
10. Parco Sempione

🕐 Ask about special tours that can get you into many non-museum sections of the castle that are normally closed to the public.

🍴 The snack vans on-site are over-priced, and the nearest bars are best avoided. Head down Via Dante to the café at no. 15, where you can enjoy panini and *gelato*.

• Map K2 • Piazza Castello, Milan; 02-8846-3700; www.milanocastello.it; 9am–7pm daily (6pm winter); free • Castle Museums: 9am–5.30pm Tue–Sun; adm €3 • Musei Civici: 02-8846-3731 or 02-8846-3636; 9am–5:30pm Tue–Sun; adm €3

1 Michelangelo's Rondanini Pietà

Michelangelo started his career with a *Pietà* carved at the age of 25 (now in St Peter's, Rome), and while the master was famous for not finishing his statues, in this instance it was not his fault. At the age of 89, in 1564, he was struck down (probably by a stroke) literally while chipping away at this sculpture *(below, right)*.

2 Funerary Monument for Gaston de Foix

Gaston de Foix was Duke of Nemours, Marshall of France, ruler of the French Milan Duchy, post-humous hero of the 1512 Battle of Ravenna and Louis XII's nephew. His tomb's ethereally sculpted elements, carved by Bambaia in 1510, are now dispersed *(see box)*.

One of the *Trivulzio Tapestries* (the month of September)

3 Sala delle Asse

The "Plank Hall" was decorated in 1498 by Leonardo da Vinci with a trompe l'oeil arbour of geometrically intricate vines on the vaulted ceiling. This was painted over many times; the only bit we can be sure is original is a mono-chrome sketch of a twisting root, on the wall between the two windows.

Mantegna's Madonna in Glory

Bellini's famous brother-in-law painted this magnificent altarpiece *(left)* for a Verona church in 1497, making it one of his final works. The harshness of his youthful style is tempered by age and experience to yield this solid, naturalistic approach.

Bellini's Madonna and Child

This is an early Bellini *(above)*, painted 1468–70, with touching detail. Mary wears a pearl-trimmed pink shawl. Jesus gazes at a lemon in his hand.

Key

▨	Ground floor
▨	First floor

Entrance

Bellini's Poet Laureate

The attribution of this portrait *(below)*, painted in 1475, has wavered between Bellini and Antonella da Messina. There is an almost Flemish attention to detail in the hair and eyes of the subject.

Trivulzio Tapestries

The *Tapestries of the Twelve Months (above)* were designed by Bramantino in 1503 and named for the man who commissioned them, General Gian Giacomo Trivulzio.

Civico Museo Archeologico

Milan's civic archaeology museum's collections go from local, Lombard artifacts of Paleolithic tribes to Italy's last Celtic peoples of the 1st century BC *(see p85)*.

Arcimboldo's Primavera

Arcimboldo developed the weird style of painting metaphoric "portraits" – in this case, using fruits and flowers to personify "Spring" as a human profile.

Parco Sempione

The 47-hectare (115-acre) park northwest of the castle is central Milan's only real green space. A public park since 1893, many of its structures are fine early 20th-century Art Nouveau *(see p85)*.

Gaston de Foix's Tomb

In 1510, King Francis I ordered a tomb for the young hero. Bambaia executed an effigy of the warrior lying in state and beautiful high relief panels. When the French pulled out of Milanese affairs in 1522, the tomb was unfinished. The pieces were sold off, winding up here, in the Ambrosiana *(see p19)*, in Turin and in London.

🔟 Pinacoteca Ambrosiana

Local Cardinal Frederico Borromeo founded this library (of some 35,000 volumes and over 750,000 prints) and painting gallery in Milan in 1603 after a formative time spent in Rome's artistic circles. It was (and is) a place in which to study theological issues via academic tomes and works of art, a truly Renaissance mix of religion, intellectualism and aesthetics. There are paintings by such greats as Tiepolo, Francesco Hayez and Jan Breughel.

The courtyard

🅞 Just around the corner from the gallery, on Via Spadari, you will find Peck *(see p68)*, one of Italy's best food emporia and oversized *tavole calde* (bars).

• Map L4 • Piazza Pio XI 2 • 02-806-921
• www.ambrosiana.it
• 10am–5:30pm Tue–Sun •
Adm €7.50, concessions €4

Top 10 Works of Art

1. Madonna del Padiglione
2. Portrait of a Musician
3. Codex Atlantico
4. Adoration of the Magi
5. Holy Family
6. Rest on the Flight into Egypt
7. Cartoon for School of Athens
8. Basket of Fruit
9. Landscape with St Paul
10. Detail from the Tomb of Gaston de Foix

1 Botticelli's Madonna del Padiglione

Angels pull back a rich canopy to reveal a scene of Mary and Jesus in a pastoral setting *(below left)*. This work dates from the 1490s, after Botticelli's religious crisis turned him from the famed mythological scenes of his brilliant youth.

2 Leonardo's Portrait of a Musician

This portrait *(right)*, quasi-Flemish in pose and detail, yet glowing with a sense of human psychology typical of Leonardo, has been said to be of various subjects, but most likely depicts a musician of the Sforza court. It is almost certainly by Leonardo, but probably retouched over the years.

Page from *Codex Atlantico*

3 Leonardo's Codex Atlantico

Reproductions of pages from these oversized tomes *(above)* reside inside glass-topped tables. They are filled with Leonardo da Vinci's sketches.

4 Titian's Adoration of the Magi

This courtly tumble of the three kings kissing the toes of baby Jesus in his manger was part of Frederico Borromeo's original collection, a complex work from 1560 that the cardinal described as "a school for painters".

5 Luini's Holy Family

If this looks familiar, it is because, especially early on, Luini was almost slavishly devoted to the manner of his master Leonardo da Vinci, and in fact this painting is based on a famous drawing by Leonardo.

6 Bassano's Rest on the Flight into Egypt

The Venetian master Jacopo Bassano was turning to a densely coloured palette, rich in contrasting tones, when he produced this work (below) in 1547.

7 Raphael's Cartoon for School of Athens

This is the preparatory drawing for Raphael's famous fresco of Greek philosophers with the faces of Renaissance artists (below).

8 Caravaggio's Basket of Fruit

This still life was probably acquired from Caravaggio by the cardinal during his Roman sojourn. The painting shows how Caravaggio was, even at the age of 25, perfecting the hyper-realism he would soon apply to large canvases and more complex scenes.

9 Bril's Landscape with St Paul

This is the most dramatic of the over half-dozen Bril works on display, showcasing how Bril managed to work with the early 17th-century's most popular sacred scenes but set them in his beloved, intricately executed landscape form.

10 Bambaia's Detail from the Tomb of Gaston de Foix

The Milanese sculptor Bambaia carved this series of small marble panels with delicate figures surrounded by military accoutrements and mythological creatures, all in extraordinary high relief. This is but a part of the work; most of the monument is in the Castello Sforzesco (see pp16–17).

Raphael's Revelation

In the final School of Athens fresco, Michelangelo (depicted as Heraclitus) lounges on the central steps. The detail is missing in this sketch because Raphael only added him when, half-way through painting, he got a glimpse of the Sistine Chapel and was deeply impressed.

🔟 Sant'Ambrogio

One of Milan's oldest basilicas (founded by St Ambrose in 379) served as a model for most of the city's early medieval churches. It was enlarged in the 9th century, and what we see today dates largely from 1080 (albeit with later reconstructions). It instantly became Milan's most beloved house of worship when the wildly popular (and future patron saint) Ambrose was buried here in 397. Everything is well signposted in Italian and English.

Nave

🔄 The best of the more portable objects formerly in the church treasury and small museum are now displayed in the Museo Diocesano *(see p93)*.

🔄 Walk northwest to the fabulous Art Nouveau café/pub Bar Magenta at Via Carducci 13 *(see p65)*.

• Map K4 • Piazza Sant'Ambrogio 15, Milan; 02-8645-0895; daily; free
• San Vittore in Ciel d'Oro: 10am–noon, 3–5pm daily; church free, museum adm €2

Top 10 Highlights

1. Atrium
2. Façade
3. Serpent Column
4. Bergognone's Redeemer
5. Sarcophagus of Stilicho
6. Pulpit
7. Golden Altar
8. Ciborium
9. Apse Mosaics
10. Sacello di San Vittore in Ciel d'Oro

1 Atrium
The first clue that this church is something apart is the lovely, elongated atrium *(below)* between the entrance and the church, built from 1088 to 1099 using columns with 6th-century capitals depicting fantastical scenes.

Façade 2
The austere but balanced façade *(right)* consists of five arches fitted under the peaked roof line. It is flanked by two mismatched towers: the Monks' Tower on the right from the 9th century and the Canons' Tower on the left from 1144.

4 Bergognone's Redeemer
This limpid, late 15th-century Renaissance scene of the Risen Christ was originally positioned on the wall to the right of the altar (where its painted trompe-l'oeil architecture was far more suited). It was later removed and placed in the first chapel on the left.

Golden altar

3 Serpent Column
Just on the inside of the third pier on the left stands a short column topped by a curlicue of a bronze serpent, a 10th-century Byzantine work (although local legend says it's the serpent cast by Moses).

6 Pulpit

This composite of 11th- and early 12th-century Romanesque relief panels was rescued after the church ceiling collapsed in 1196 and reconstructed into this magnificent pulpit *(left)*.

5 Sarcophagus of Stilicho

This late Roman-era sarcophagus *(above)* preceded the pulpit (No. 6) built around it. The tomb is aligned with the original walls, while the pulpit is aligned with the nave.

7 Golden Altar

A master goldsmith, Volvinio, crafted the "golden altar" in 835 *(below)*. The Life of Christ is in gold leaf on the front, and the Life of St Ambrose in gilded silver on the back.

Plan of Basilica

Entrance

8 Ciborium

This altar canopy *(below)* sits at the centre of the presbytery. Its four ancient Roman columns support a canopy of four 10th-century Lombard polychrome stucco reliefs.

St Ambrose

Ambrose (340–97) became Archbishop of Milan in 374, where he set about building the four great basilicas (this church, San Lorenzo, San Nazaro and San Sempliciano), tutoring St Augustine (whom he baptized into Christianity), and generally controlling the city from his bishop's throne. He was canonized soon after his death and became the city's patron.

9 Apse Mosaics

The vast, colourful mosaic depicting Christ Pantocrater *(above)* was largely pieced together between the 4th and 8th centuries, though bits were touched up or redone between the 17th and 20th centuries, especially after a 1943 bombing tore away half of Christ and the Archangel on the left.

10 Sacello di San Vittore in Ciel d'Oro

Sant'Ambrogio was built next to a Paleochristian cemetery and a chapel decorated in the 5th century with a glittering dome of almost solid gold mosaics. The basilica grew to include the chapel and its ancient mosaics.

🔟 Lake Maggiore's Isole Borromee

This trio of islets – Isola Bella ("Beautiful Island"), Isola Madre ("Mother Island") and Isola Superiore, or Isola dei Pescatori ("Isle of the Fishermen") – has been shaped by the Borromeo family, who in the 16th and 17th centuries turned Bella and Madre into vast garden-and-palace complexes. If you've time only for one, make it Isola Bella, though its ornate, formal gardens are less relaxing and botanically interesting than Isola Madre's.

Isola Madre gardens

⭐ Buy discounted island admission tickets along with your ferry ticket at the Stresa docks.

Isola Bella's gardens remain open all day, but access is via the Palazzo so you can't enter between noon and 1:30pm.

📷 There are many cafés on Isola Bella's quay. Café Lago serves sandwiches, coffee and lager to a backdrop of rock music.

- Map A2
- Access is from the ferry docks at Stresa (see p99) • www. borromeoturismo.it
- Isola Bella 0323-30-556; 22 Mar–26 Oct: 9am–5:30pm (Oct until 5pm) daily; adm €10, under-16s €4.50
- Isola Madre 0323-31-261; 22 Mar–26 Oct: 9am–5:30pm (Oct until 5pm) daily; adm €9, under-16s €4.50

Top 10 Highlights

1. Isola Bella: Borromeo Palace
2. Isola Bella: Sala di Musica in the Palace
3. Isola Bella: Tapestries in the Palace
4. Isola Bella: Grottoes
5. Isola Bella: Borromeo Tombs
6. Isola Bella: Gardens
7. Isola Madre: Villa Borromeo
8. Isola Madre: Botanical Gardens
9. Isola Madre: Kashmir Cypress
10. Isola Superiore

1 Isola Bella: Borromeo Palace
The vast Borromeo Palace and its grounds *(below)* dominate the island. The palace is largely 17th century, but wasn't finished until 1959. The sumptuous rooms have stucco ceilings and are filled with inlaid dressers, Murano chandeliers and fine paintings.

4 Isola Bella: Grottoes
Artificial caves were all the rage in the 18th century *(above)*. They were decorated with a sort of grand, intricate pebble-dash in black-and-white patterns.

Isola Bella Gardens

2 Isola Bella: Sala di Musica in the Palace
The palace's most important room is named for its collection of antique instruments. On 11 April 1935, Mussolini met here with Laval of France and Ramsay MacDonald of Britain in an attempt to stave off World War II.

3 Isola Bella: Tapestries in the Palace
This detail-rich series of 16th-century Flemish works is based on that popular theme for medieval tapestries: the unicorn (which is also a Borromeo heraldic totem).

5 Isola Bella: Borromeo Tombs

The "Private Chapel" was built in 1842–4 as a mausoleum for a pair of late Gothic/early Renaissance 15th-century family tombs as well as the 1522 Monument to the Birago Brothers, carved by Renaissance master Bambaia.

6 Isola Bella: Gardens

This pyramid of terraces *(left)* is topped by a unicorn, the edges lined by statue-laden balustrades. A few pairs of white peacocks strut over the clipped lawns.

7 Isola Madre: Villa Borromeo

This summer villa was built largely between 1518 and 1585. Today it is a museum with mannequins in Borromeo livery and paraphernalia from puppet theatres.

8 Isola Madre: Botanical Gardens

The surprisingly lush and extensive gardens *(above)* around the Villa Borromeo are filled with exotic flora. Take the time to walk around the island, past the azaleas, rhododendrons and camellias famous since the 19th century.

9 Isola Madre: Kashmir Cypress

Europe's largest cypress spreads its 200-year-old, weeping Oriental strands of needles over a gravel courtyard to one side of the Villa Borromeo.

10 Isola Superiore

The Borromei pretty much left this island (also known as Isola dei Pescatori, *right*) alone when they were converting its neighbours into sumptuous garden-palaces, allowing the island's fishing hamlet to develop more naturally into a tourist draw today.

The Borromeo Family

The Borromeo clan fled political intrigue in Tuscany for Milan in 1395, where they bankrolled the rise of the Visconti. Building a pan-European financial empire, they bought the Arona fiefdom in 1447. They skilfully tacked through the era's turbulent political winds, married wisely, and associated with the Sforza while slowly acquiring control of Lake Maggiore. The family still owns the islands.

 For a day's itinerary including Isole Borromee see p101

⁜10 Certosa di Pavia

Gian Galeazzo Visconti founded this charterhouse in 1396 as a vast family mausoleum, set 8 km (5 miles) north of Pavia. Finished in the mid-16th century under the Sforzas, it became one of the great monuments of the Lombard Renaissance. After the 1782 suppression of the Carthusian order, it was abandoned, then inhabited for brief spells until, in 1968, the Cistercians moved in to stay.

Façade of charterhouse

➊ Avoid visiting at the weekend, when the sight is very crowded.

To get past the elaborate 1660 iron screen at the end of the nave, wait until one of the monks escorts a small group in to see the famous tombs and cloisters.

➋ There's nowhere to eat near the Certosa, so either head into Pavia itself, or bring a picnic and buy some of the monks' liqueur.

• Map C5 • Via del Monumento 4, Pavia • 9–11:30am Tue–Sun; and Apr, Sep: 2:30–5:30pm; May–Aug: 2:30–6pm; Oct, Mar: 2:30–5pm; Nov–Feb: 2:30–4:30pm
• Free • For more details, contact Pavia's tourist office: 0382-597-001

Top 10 Highlights

1. Façade
2. Perugino's Altarpiece
3. Bergognone's Works
4. St Ambrose with Saints
5. Funerary Monument of Ludovico il Moro and Beatrice d'Este
6. Ivory Altar
7. Tomb of Gian Galeazzo Visconti
8. Great Cloister
9. Little Cloister
10. Monks' Shop

1 Façade

The astounding and rich façade *(above left)* has decorative flourishes and polychrome marbles that set it apart and make it one of Italy's most important and idiosyncratic examples of late 15th-century architecture. The initial work was undertaken in 1473–99; the top part was continued after 1525, but never finished.

2 Perugino's Altarpiece

The central panel *(left)* of the *Eternal Father* (1499) is all that remains here of the original full altarpiece by Umbrian master (and Raphael's first teacher) Perugino. The flanking panels are by Bergognone, while below are 16th-century reproductions of the other, original Perugino panels.

The Little Cloister

3 Bergognone's Works

Bergognone rules the Certosa, providing altarpieces for three chapels, plus part of Perugino's altarpiece. He also frescoed the seventh chapel on the right *(detail, above)* and the ends of both transepts, brilliantly blue with lapis lazuli.

4 St Ambrose with Saints

In Bergognone's 1492 altarpiece in the sixth chapel on the left, St Ambrose is enthroned and surrounded by four saints. The group is in a setting similar to the chapel interior, to create the illusion that they are present.

\\Entrance

5 Funerary Monument of Ludovico il Moro and Beatrice d'Este

The most renowned work in the Certosa is an empty tomb *(see box)*, with remarkably lifelike effigies of the couple *(above, right)* lying in state, carved in 1497 by Cristoforo Solari.

7 Tomb of Gian Galeazzo Visconti

It's only fitting that the Certosa's founder should be buried here, in a monument of 1492–7 depicting scenes from Visconti's life, carved by Gian Cristoforo Romano. The sarcophagus below is by Andrea Alessi, while the statues of the *Virgin*, *Fame* and *Victory* were added in the mid-16th century.

9 Little Cloister

Guiniforte Solari designed this lovely arcaded space for the monks to gather and contemplate – and probably admire the magnificent flank of the church above.

6 Ivory Altar

The Florentine sculptor Baldassare degli Embriachi carved this ivory triptych altarpiece (1400–1409), with 76 compartments and more than 100 tiny statues. It was stolen in 1984, leading to the uncovering of a ring of international art thieves outside Naples. The treasure, slightly damaged, was recovered.

A Peripatetic Tomb

The sad story behind the beautiful tomb of Ludovico il Moro and his wife Beatrice d'Este illustrates that even the best-laid plans of the mightiest men can go terribly awry. The duke and his wife were meant to be buried together in Milan's Santa Maria delle Grazie (where the *Last Supper* had just been painted). But Ludovico ended up dying in exile in France, so only Beatrice was buried in Milan, and the church, strapped for cash, sold the funerary monument to the Certosa in 1564.

8 Great Cloister

This large arcaded cloister *(below)* is lined with the homes of the Cistercian monks who still inhabit the Certosa. These are cosy little two-storey houses with a tiny private chapel and walled gardens at the back.

10 Monks' Shop

The Cistercian monks make their own Chartreuse liqueurs, herbal soaps and scents, which they sell here to the public.

For more on Pavia town see p46

25

🔟 Bergamo

One of Northern Italy's surprising gems, Bergamo mixes medieval charm with a cultural sophistication that has made it popular among Italy's cognoscenti. Bergamo has been a split-level town since Roman times, when a civitas (today's medieval Upper Town) perched atop the hill and a suburbia (the modernized Lower Town) spread into the plain.

Baptistry

🔵 To get to the Upper Town from the train station, take bus 1 or 1A and transfer (free) to the Funicolare Bergamo Alta.

🔵 The Caffè del Funiculare has sweeping views over the valley, and over 50 beers and 100 whiskies *(see also pp128–9).*

• Map D3
• Tourist info: IAT, www. comune.bergamo.it
• Piazzale Marconi, 035-210-204 • Viale Gombito 13 (Upper Town), 035-242-226

• Basilica 9am–noon (until 1pm Sun), 3–6pm daily; free
• Museo Donizettiano 9:30am–1pm, 2–5:30pm Tue–Sun; Oct–Mar: closed weekday afternoons; free
• Castello 9am–dusk daily; free
• Galleria d'Arte 10am–7pm Tue–Sun; adm €6
• Galleria dell'Accademia Carrara 9:30am–1pm, 2:30–6:45pm Tue–Sun (Oct–Mar: to 5:45pm); adm €6

Top 10 Sights

1. Piazza del Duomo
2. Piazza Vecchia
3. Cappella Colleoni
4. Basilica di Santa Maria Maggiore
5. Museo Donizettiano
6. Via Colleoni
7. Castello
8. Galleria d'Arte Moderna e Contemporanea
9. Galleria dell'Accademia Carrara
10. Teatro Donizetti

1 Piazza del Duomo

This square is dominated by elaborate Bergamasco architecture: the entrance to Santa Maria Maggiore, the façade of the Capella Colleoni and a fanciful baptistery *(above left)* of 1340.

2 Piazza Vecchia

One of Northern Italy's most theatrical squares *(above, right)* is surrounded by retro-medieval stone buildings, Renaissance palaces, a 12th-century tower and several historic cafés.

Piazza Vecchia

3 Cappella Colleoni

The anchor of the twinned Piazzas Vecchia and del Duomo is this magnificent Renaissance chapel *(left)* devoted to Bergamo's warrior-lord Bartolomeo Colleoni. In pink and white patterned marble, it is covered with reliefs and Rococo frescoes.

4 Basilica di Santa Maria Maggiore

Inside the basilica *(left)*, every inch of ceiling is covered with frescoes. Against the back wall is the tomb of composer Gaetano Donizetti. The gorgeous, early 16th-century, inlaid wood panels fronting the choir are by Lorenzo Lotto.

7 LARGO COLLE APERTO

Bergamo

6 P. D. BOCCOLA · VIA DELLA FARA
PIAZZA MASCHERONI · PZA. MERC. DEL FIENO
ⓘ
5 **1** **2** · PZA. MERC. DEL SCARPE · VIA PORTA DIPINTA · VIALE D. MURA
3 **4**
9
PIAZZA CARRARA **8**
10 · VIA V. EMANUELE II

5 Museo Donizettiano

Here are the original sheet music, piano *(left)* and memorabilia of Bergamo's early 19th-century composer Gaetano Donizetti. He died, in the very bed on display here, of syphilis in 1848.

6 Via Colleoni

The main drag of Bergamo's Upper Town is lined with shops and wine bars, modest medieval palaces and churches, tiny squares and half-timbered houses. It's closed to most traffic, and filled every evening with hordes of locals and visitors.

7 Castello

Built by the town's Venetian lords in the 16th and 17th centuries, the castle in the hamlet of San Vigilio on Bergamo's hill has been reduced to the romantically decrepit ruins you can see today, with a public garden boasting fine views.

8 Galleria d'Arte Moderna e Contemporanea

Bergamo's modern art gallery features exhibitions alongside a permanent collection with works by some of Italy's key 20th-century painters: Giovanni Fattori, Boccioni, De Chirico, and Morandi as well as some Kandinskys.

9 Galleria dell' Accademia Carrara

This excellent gallery is renowned for its outstanding works by early 16th-century master Lorenzo Lotto. Paintings by Raphael, Botticelli *(above)*, Bellini and Mantegna round out the collections.

10 Teatro Donizetti

Although the façade dates from 1897, this respected theatre was built in 1792, and the Neo-Classical interiors are wonderfully preserved. It has an annual opera season, plus ballet and drama.

The Lower Town

Few visitors make it to the open, spacious streets of the Lower Town, laid out largely in the 20th century (but settled since Roman times). The chief boulevard of this vibrant area is the Sentierone ("big path"). This is where most Bergamaschi head of an evening to shop in the stores and meet at the cafés.

🔟 Mantova

This town is known for its fine palaces, its masterpieces by Mantegna and Giulio Romano and its position surrounded on three sides by wide, shallow, swamp-edged lakes. These man-made lakes make the area humid in summer and rather damp and chilly in winter, creating a slight air of melancholy. The poet Virgil was born here in 70 BC. By 1328, the town had come under the rule of the Gonzagas, who held onto the reigns of power until the Austrians took over in 1707.

Fresco in the Chamber of the Wind, Palazzo Te

🚲 Meander like a true Mantovano: hire a bicycle from La Rigola, on Lungolago dei Gonzaga.

☕ Caffè Miró is on the tiny piazza in front of Sant'Andrea (see also pp128–9).

• Map H6 • Tourist info: Piazza Mantegna 6
• 0376-432-432 • www.turismo.mantova.it
• Duomo 7am–noon, 3–7pm daily; free
• Palazzo Ducale 8:45am–7:15pm Tue–Sun; adm €6.50
• Sant'Andrea 8am–noon, 3–7pm daily; free
• Rotonda 10am–1pm, 3–6pm Mon–Fri, 10am–6pm Sat, Sun; donation
• Teatro Bibiena 9:30am–12:30pm, 3–6pm Tue–Sun; adm €2
• Palazzo d'Arco 10am–12:30pm, 2:30–6pm Tue–Sun; adm €3
• Casa del Mantegna 9am–12:30pm Mon–Fri, 3–6pm Mon & Thu; free
• Palazzo Te 9am–6pm Tue–Sun, 1–6pm Mon; adm €8

Top 10 Sights

1. Duomo
2. Palazzo Ducale
3. Piazza Broletto
4. Piazza delle Erbe
5. Basilica di Sant'Andrea
6. Rotunda di San Lorenzo
7. Teatro Scientifico Bibena
8. Palazzo d'Arco
9. Casa del Mantegna
10. Palazzo Te

1 Duomo

Fire claimed the Gothic cathedral. The façade *(right)* is late Baroque (1756–61), and Giulio Romano's interior was designed in imitation of Paleochristian basilicas.

Duomo, Piazza Sordello

2 Palazzo Ducale

Highlights in the Gonzagas' rambling fortress-palace *(above)* include tapestries by Raphael and Mantegna's *Camera degli Sposi* frescoes (1465–74).

3 Piazza Broletto

Just north of the arcaded Piazza delle Erbe is this tiny square hemmed in by medieval buildings, including the 1227 *broletto* (town hall).

4 Piazza delle Erbe

Piazza delle Erbe *(below)* is a wonderfully jumbled, lively urban space, lined by arcades, filled with a food market each morning, and ringed by a fascinating assemblage of buildings.

5 Basilica di Sant'Andrea

Lodovico Gonzaga commissioned this glorious basilica *(left)* in 1470 from Leon Battista Alberti, its façade a highly original take on Classicism. Mantegna is buried in the first chapel on the left.

6 Rotonda di San Lorenzo

This rotund church is a relic from an earlier age, built in 1082 and retaining scraps of medieval fresco in its otherwise pleasantly bare brick interior.

7 Teatro Scientifico Bibiena

This jewel-box of a late Baroque theatre is named after the architect who designed it, and was inaugurated in 1770 with a concert by Mozart, then a 13-year-old prodigy.

8 Palazzo d'Arco

This Neo-Classically remodelled *palazzo* from the Renaissance includes the 1520 Sala dello Zodiaco, frescoed with astrological signs, in an original 15th-century wing.

9 Casa del Mantegna

Mantova's most famous artist, Andrea Mantegna (1431–1506), custom-built this house-and-studio in 1465–74. It includes a circular courtyard *(left)* and a portrait of himself by his fellow-artist and friend Titian.

10 Palazzo Te

Giulio Romano's Mannerist masterpiece *(right)* is an ingenious interplay of spacious courts, sweeping building wings and discreet gardens. Built in 1525, it was frescoed largely by Romano.

Boat Tours

The Gonzagas widened the Mincio River, cupping their city within three defensive lakes. Lined by reeds, floating with white lotus, and now the protected homes of waterfowl and the highest concentration of fish in Italy, they're at their best in late May and June. You can take boat tours with Negrini, Via San Giorgio 2 (0376-322-875) or Motonavi River Queen (0425-893-61).

Left **Pope Alexander III meets Barbarossa** Right **Benito Mussolini**

TOP 10 Moments in History

1 298–283 BC: Third Samnite War

The Po Valley and land to the north, once called Cisalpine Gaul, was a Celtic province that often found itself up against Rome. Its alliance with the Samnites failed, and Rome used the excuse to push its boundary north of the Po.

2 AD 313: Edict of Milan

During Rome's decline Milan became de facto capital of the Western Empire. Constantine, holding court here in 313, made Christianity the Empire's official religion, setting a new course for European history.

3 572: Fall of Pavia to Lombards

In the 5th century barbarian tribes overran the disintegrating Roman Empire. Most came, sacked and left, but the Germanic Lombards took Pavia in 572 and settled in the Po Valley, expanding across the north. Eventually the Byzantines and Charlemagne trounced them, and the region dissolved into a network of city-

states that lasted throughout the Middle Ages.

4 1176: Lombard League Defeats Barbarossa

When Swabian Emperor Frederick I (Barbarossa) levelled Milan and set up his own puppet mayors, the region's happily self-governing cities banded together as the Lombard League and with papal support forced Barbarossa to return their autonomy.

5 1277: Ottone Visconti Defeats the Torriani

Archbishop Visconti overthrew the leading Torriani family in 1277. Under 160 years of Visconti rule, Milan extended its hegemony over much of the north.

6 1450: Francesco Sforza Comes to Power

The last Visconti died in 1447, leaving only an illegitimate daughter who couldn't inherit the title but was married to one Francesco Sforza. Milan's young Ambrosian Republic rashly hired Sforza to defend them from Venetian power-grabbers. Instead, he cut a deal with Venice, split up the territory and made himself duke.

7 1499: The Sforza Cede Milan to France

Francesco's son Galeazzo Maria was murdered in 1476,

Francesco Sforza comes to power in 1450

  Previous pages **Leonardo's *Last Supper* (see pp8–9)**

after which power passed to Galeazzo's brother Lodovico, who was known as "Il Moro" ("The Moor") on account of his looks. Lodovico ushered the Renaissance into Milan, inviting the likes of Leonardo da Vinci to his court, but in 1499 ceded control to Louis XII. The city changed hands repeatedly until Austria seized power in 1706.

8 1848: Cinque Giornate Revolt

The 19th-century Risorgimento (unification movement) inspired the Milanese to rise up, on March 18, for five days, with their victory triggering the demise of Austrian rule. By 1859 King Vittorio Emanuele II controlled Lombardy: he sent General Garibaldi off to conquer the rest of the peninsula, forming a new kingdom – Italy.

9 1945: Mussolini Executed

Mussolini's fascist regime ended after his alliance with Hitler put Italy on the losing side of World War II. As the Allies drew closer Mussolini fled with his mistress. They were caught by partisans and shot on Lake Como, their bodies later strung up on Milan's Piazzale Loreto and stoned.

10 1990: Lombard League Wins Local Elections

Northern resentment of sharing wealth with the considerably poorer south found political expression in the Lombard League, a separatist party that came to prominence in 1990. Re-dubbed the Northern League, the party espoused federalism and in 2001 gained power as part of the Forza Italia coalition led by media mogul and entrepreneur Silvio Berlusconi.

Top 10 Historical Figures

1 St Ambrose (334–97) Milan's bishop put down the Arian heresy and helped establish Church autonomy.

2 St Augustine (354–430) St Ambrose's star pupil – an African-born philosopher.

3 Theodolinda (500s) Lombard queen who converted her populace to orthodox Christianity.

4 Gian Galeazzo Visconti (1378–1402) This conqueror of vast territories was the first Milan ruler to gain the title of Duke.

5 Lodovico "Il Moro" Sforza (1452–1508) "The Moor" ruled Milan's Renaissance court but ceded to France, later siding against the French and being exiled.

6 St Charles Borromeo (1538–84) The crusading archbishop carried out Counter-Reformation ideals in the north.

7 Antonio Stradivari (1644–1737) The greatest violin-maker who ever lived learned his craft in the city of Cremona.

8 Alessandro Volta (1745–1827) This Como physicist invented the battery in 1800 and gave his name to the electrical unit.

9 Antonio di Pietro (b. 1950) The Christian Democrat party collapsed in 1992 following this magistrate's investigation into political corruption.

10 Silvio Berlusconi (b. 1936) The founder of the Forza Italia party survived bribery scandals to serve as prime minister in 1994 and from 2001.

Left **La Scala poster** Centre **Haute couture shopping** Right **Panini snacks at the bar**

Lombard Experiences

Detail of the Duomo's rooftop

1 Exploring the Roof of Milan's Duomo

You can wander freely about the forest of Gothic carving adorning the rooftop of Milan's cathedral. Duck under the buttresses, skirt along the eaves and clamber onto the peaked roof of the nave to drink in a panorama across the city (see pp10–11).

2 A Milanese Shopping Spree

Milan is a world capital of high fashion, home to dozens of the top names in haute couture (see pp58–9) in its Quadrilatero d'Oro, or "Golden Rectangle" of streets (see p57). Add in designer household objects, silk from Como, fine wines and foods, and Milan becomes a shopper's paradise.

3 Snacking on a Café Crawl

After 5pm or so, many Milanese bars and cafés practise the lovely habit of laying out platters of mini-sandwiches, canapés, olives, crisps and other snacks at the bar, all free for the munching as long as you order at least one drink. You can easily flit from one bar to the next, and make a decent early dinner out of it all.

4 An Evening on the Navigli

Milan's southern district of canals and warehouses has been converted to a lively evening area of restaurants, pizzerias, bars, pubs and funky shops (see p94).

Cruise boat, Lake Como

Milan's Navigli district

5 A Night at the Opera
Italy's premier opera house, La Scala, has now emerged from extensive restoration, and you can again enjoy one of the world's best companies in a truly wondrous 18th-century setting *(see p74)*.

6 A Violin Concert in Cremona
In the city where Amati honed his craft and passed his skills to Stradivari, they take their fiddling seriously. Virtuosos from around the globe come to numerous festivals, concert seasons and trade fairs just for the chance to bow a few sonatas on the city's vast collection of original Strads *(see also p127)*.

7 A Cruise on Lake Como
The loveliest of the Italian lakes *(see pp106–113)* is best enjoyed from the waters. From this vantage point, devoid of traffic jams, you can see the glorious gardens and gracious villas lining its banks (from the road, all you may see is a high wall).

8 Sports on Lake Garda
The northern end of Lake Garda is buffeted by strong winds blowing down from the Sarca Valley in the north in morning (the *sover*) and south up the lake in the afternoon (the *ora*). Together, they make for some of the best windsurfing and sailing conditions on any lake in Western Europe, and all summer long watersports fans flock from far and wide to Riva and its neighbour Torbole to thrash the waves *(see also p120)*.

9 Hill-Walking near the Lakes
Local tourist offices can often supply maps of mountain trails ranging from 15 minutes to two hours or more. Pick a point of interest as a goal: a ruined castle

Windsurfing on Lake Garda

(Arco on Garda, Varenna on Como), medieval church (Madonna del Sasso above Locarno on Maggiore, San Pietro above Civate on Como), surging mountain stream (Lattefiume above Lake Como's Varenna, Cascata del Varone above Riva del Garda), or prehistoric rock carvings *(below)*.

10 Seeking out the Region's Rock Carvings
The prehistoric Camuni tribes etched many rock faces in the pre-Alpine valleys of eastern Lombardy with curious figurative images and symbols. The oldest date back 11,000 years, while the most recent are medieval. Most carvings are in the Val Calmonica *(see p47)*. However, if you're on Lake Garda, detour at Torri del Benaco to the hillside hamlet of Crer, where a trail leads to some nice carvings.

Left **Casa degli Omenoni** Centre **Ca' Grande** Right **Entrance to the Galleria Vittorio Emanuele II**

Notable Milanese Buildings

1 Palazzo Litta
This 1648 *palazzo* got a Rococo makeover in 1763. Today it houses the state railway offices (though they have long planned a move), a theatre and a Louis XV-style apartment open during special events and exhibitions *(see p88)*.

Torre Velasca

2 Palazzo della Ragione
The arcade that takes up the ground level of this Lombard Romanesque palace, built in 1228–33 (the top floor dates from 1771), once hosted the city's main market. The relief on the façade depicts the 13th-century mayor Oldrado da Tresseno on horseback. Inside, the Salone dei Giudici has its original frescoes *(see p73)*.

3 Torre Velasca
When Nathan Rogers, Lodovico Belgioioso and Enrico Peressutti constructed this brick-red, 106-m (348-ft) tower block in 1956–8, they showcased their post-war engineering talents by extending the top nine floors beyond the lower ones on struts, much like an oversized medieval tower. Unfortunately, the maintenance costs have proved to be horrendous *(see p76)*.

4 Ca' Grande
In 1456 Francesco Sforza instituted one of his greatest public works, a massive hospital with separate wings for women and men, each based around four courtyards. The vast central Cortile Maggiore was added in the 17th century, along with the Annunciazione church with its Guercino altarpiece. The Neo-Classical men's wing was eventually completed in 1804; but the entire hospital moved elsewhere in 1939, to be replaced by the University of Milan in 1958 *(see p76)*.

5 Galleria Vittorio Emanuele II
High-class Italian elegance came to terms with the Industrial Age in such marvels of engineering as this four-storey shopping arcade roofed with a steel-and-glass canopy. It was built in

Galleria Vittorio Emanuele II

1864–8 by Giuseppe Mengoni, who fell to his death from its scaffolding just days before the King arrived to open the galleria and lend it his name *(see p74)*.

6 Palazzo Marino

Milan's *municipio* (city hall) has two distinct façades: a 1553 Mannerist one on Piazza S Fedele, and an 1886–92 Neo-Classical one facing La Scala theatre. The former was built by Galeazzo Alessi (who also designed the lovely main courtyard) in 1558; the latter dates to 1860 *(see p76)*.

7 Casa degli Omenoni

Renaissance sculptor Leone Leoni, whose works grace Milan's Duomo and Madrid's El Escorial, built this *palazzo* in 1565, lining the lower level of the façade with eight giant telamones – columns in the form of a male figure *(see p76)*.

8 Palazzo Dugnani

The Salone d'Onore in this late 17th-century *palazzo* is a vast chamber with a cast-iron balcony. The 1731 ceiling was frescoed by Gian Battista Tiepolo with allegorical scenes glorifying the Dugnani family. A modest Museo del Cinema, which traces the early history of cinema, is housed in the building *(see p88)*.

9 Pirelli Tower

Milan once had a rule about structures rising no higher than the golden Madonnina atop the Duomo *(see p11)*. The 127.1-m (417-ft) Pirelli Tower – designed in 1955–60 by a team headed by Gio Ponti and including Pier Luigi Nervi

Stazione Centrale

– broke that tradition, but placed a replica of the Madonnina on its own roof so she would still have the highest vantage point in Milan. It now houses Lombardy's regional government and in 2002 survived being struck by a small plane *(see p88)*.

10 Stazione Centrale

Milan's massive railway station is often considered a remarkable example of Fascist-era architecture, though its design (of 1912) pre-dates this period and owes more to the Liberty style. Finally completed in 1931, the station is caked in gleaming white Aurisina stone and decorated with reliefs, statues and murals too often overlooked. ◈ *Piazza Duca D'Aosta*

Left **Baptistry, Bergamo** Centre **Sant'Eustorgio, Milan** Right **Certosa di Pavia**

🔟 Churches

1 Duomo, Milan

Milan's cathedral is the third-largest church in the world and a testament to Milanese persistence. Despite construction that lasted more than 400 years (1386–1813), it managed to remain uncompromisingly faithful to the original Gothic design, a beautiful hulk of stone turrets, statues and flying buttresses *(see pp10–11)*.

Duomo, Milan

2 Sant'Ambrogio, Milan

St Ambrose himself, Milan's 4th-century bishop, inaugurated this church, which was overhauled in the 11th and 12th centuries. Highlights include a quiet entry atrium, Dark-Age mosaics glittering in the apse, and medieval features *(see pp20–21)*.

3 San Lorenzo Maggiore, Milan

Dating from the 4th century, this church is still pretty much Roman in its rotund design, although it was rebuilt several times in the Middle Ages. Inside the church are some of the oldest and best-preserved examples of post-Roman art in Northern Italy: 1,600-year-old Paleochristian mosaics *(see also p93)*.

4 Santa Maria delle Grazie, Milan

Each year, hundreds of thousands of people visit Leonardo da Vinci's *Last Supper* fresco in the adjacent refectory *(see pp8–9)*, but only a few bother with the lovely church itself. Make the effort, though, if you can: its architecture shows the stylistic changeover, from austere Gothic to Classical Renaissance, that marked the end of the 15th century. The art here is among Milan's best in sculpture, fresco and the rare *sgraffito* (etched designs) recently restored in the tribune *(see also p85)*.

5 Santa Maria presso San Satiro, Milan

Though the main entrance is on Via Torino, walk around and up Via Speronari to see an 11th-century bell tower and the pretty exterior of a tiny Renaissance

Sant'Ambrogio, Milan

chapel. Turn right again on Via Falcone for the Renaissance-meets-Baroque rear façade finished in 1871. Here a secondary entrance is usually open, so you can nip inside to admire the 15th-century decorations *(see also p73)*.

6 Sant'Eustorgio, Milan
Ignore the insipid 19th-century façade, for the church behind it is ancient, founded in the 4th century. Beyond the main church and behind the altar is the cappella Portinari. It was designed locally, but so superbly did it embody early Renaissance Florentine ideals that it was for a long time attributed to Brunelleschi or Michelozzo. The chapel's master-pieces are the 1486 frescoes by Vicenzo Foppa *(see also p94)*.

7 Certosa di Pavia
Gian Galeazzo Visconti commissioned the construction of this vast, gorgeous Charterhouse in 1396 as a lavishly decorated home for a group of Carthusian monks, but more importantly to ensure his ruling clan would have a family burial chapel of gargan-tuan proportions and extravagant artistic merit *(see p24–5)*.

8 Cappella Colleoni, Bergamo
Bartolomeo Colleoni was a *condottiere*, a redoubtable mercenary general who, as a reward for his services, received Bergamo as his own fiefdom. Never much of a one for understatement, Colleoni demolished a church sacristy to make his own tomb, hiring the sculptor Amadeo to decorate it with a complex

Duomo, Como

allegory of Biblical and Classical reliefs plus a horse-mounted effigy of himself for the sepulchre inside *(see also p26)*.

9 Duomo, Como
Como's statue-studded cathedral is devoted to local pat-ron and protector Sant'Abbondio, whose life is played out in the giant gilt altarpiece of 1509–14. Other Renaissance tapestries and paintings – including one by Leonardo's protégé Bernardino Luini – grace the interior *(see also p107)*.

10 Basilica di Sant'Andrea, Mantova
Sant'Andrea, Mantova

Built to house a vial of Christ's blood, this basilica was created by some of Italy's finest architectural talents. Leon Battista Alberti, the great Renaissance theorist, designed it in 1470, Giulio Romano, a founder of Mannerism, enlarged it in 1530, and Baroque master Juvarra added the dome in 1732. Frescoes cover every inch of the barrel-vaulted interior *(see also p29)*.

Left **Pinacoteca di Brera** Centre **Castello Sforzesco** Right **Museo Nazionale della Scienza**

🔟 Museums

1 Pinacoteca di Brera, Milan
Lombardy's most important painting gallery, displaying works by Mantegna, Giovanni Bellini, Piero della Francesca, Caravaggio, Tintoretto, Veronese, Coreggio, Lotto, Carpaccio, Tiepolo, El Greco and Rembrandt *(see pp12–15)*.

2 Pinacoteca Ambrosiana, Milan
This formidable mix of Old Masters was started by Cardinal Federico Borromeo as an adjunct to the Ambrosiana Library. Famously, the library is home to the *Codex Atlantico*, which contains the lion's share of Leonardo's drawings and sketches – photocopied pages from it are displayed in the Pinacoteca. Elsewhere, you'll find paintings by Botticelli, Titian and Caravaggio, as well as Raphael's giant preparatory sketch for the *School of Athens (see pp18–19)*.

3 Castello Sforzesco, Milan
The greatest free museum in Italy! There's a bit of everything: paintings by the likes of Bellini and Mantegna, a cycle of 16th-

Pinacoteca Ambrosiana, Milan

century tapestries, archaeological collections and, its greatest piece, Michelangelo's unfinished *Rondanini Pietà (see pp16–17)*. Within the castle are the Musei Civici, which charge an entry fee.

4 Museo Poldi-Pezzoli, Milan
Poldi-Pezzoli's mansion is preserved as a monument to his collections, from Persian tapestries, ancient arms and armour to historic jewellery and, above all, art. In one room alone, there are paintings by Piero della Francesca, Giovanni Bellini, Mantegna and Botticelli *(see p74)*.

5 Museo Nazionale della Scienza e della Tecnica – Leonardo da Vinci, Milan
Had Leonardo possessed more technological ambition, we might have had working versions of his helicopters, water screws, gatling guns, parachutes and siege engines over four centuries ago. As it is, we can make do with the (modern) wooden mock-ups on display at this science and technology museum, alongside instructive exhibits on physics and antique autos and aeroplanes *(see p93)*.

6 Civico Museo Archeologico, Milan
Among the top pieces in this small archaeological collection, which traces Lombard and neighbouring civilizations from prehistory to the end of the Roman era,

Set design by Giacoma Balla, Museo Teatrale alla Scala, Milan

and art, left his collection to Bergamo on his death in 1796. Today the gallery houses over 1,800 paintings, including works by Botticelli, Mantegna, Bellini and Raffaello. There is also a significant collection of prints and sketches, sculpture and china. Above all, though, come to admire the emotion-filled Renaissance paintings of Lorenzo Lotto, a Venetian painter who settled in Bergamo in 1513 (see pp26–7).

is the Trivulzio Cup. This precious 4th-century glass cup has a delicate glass netting hovering just above the chalice surface on thin stilts of glass, along with a raised inscription that reads "Drink to Enjoy Long Life" (see p85).

7 Museo Teatrale alla Scala, Milan

If it has to do with the opera in Milan, it's on display here. It's an odd collection, from costumes worn by Nureyev or Callas to historic musical instruments, and from Verdi's death mask (and some of his original scores) to Toscanini's batons (see p88).

8 Civico Museo d'Arte Contemporanea, Milan

Milan's gallery of modern art is among the best in Italy. The works concentrate on Italian artists of the 20th century, including De Chirico, Modigliani and Boccioni. The collection is housed in the Palazzo Reale (see p73). The museum underwent restoration in 2004. Call ahead to confirm opening hours.

9 Galleria dell'Accademia Carrara, Bergamo

Count Giacomo Carrara, a collector and expert on literature

10 Museo della Città, Brescia

Though there are Romanesque carvings and detached frescoes galore in the cloisters, chapels and chambers of this medieval monastery, the real focus here is on Brescia's great era as a Roman colony, and the archaeological works on display are astoundingly beautiful, numerous and well preserved (see also p126).

Lotto's Mystic Marriage of St Catherine

Left **The town of Bellagio on Lake Como** Right **Sirmione**

🔟 Lakeside Attractions

1 Isole Borromee, Lake Maggiore

This trio of islets off Stresa – two clad in gardens and palaces, the third with a fishing village – rank among the top 10 sights in the whole region *(see pp22–3).*

Rocca di Anghera

servicing the ancient dock are infrequent. Look out on the loggia for a winch assembly once used with a basket to raise the daily shopping – and the occasional frail monk – from the boat decks *(see also p99).*

2 Santa Caterina del Sasso, Lake Maggiore

The façade and interior of this church perched just above the water are covered with decaying frescoes dating from the hermitage's foundation in the 13th century to its suppression by the Austrians in the 19th; the Dominicans returned in 1986. Be warned: there are many steps down from the car park, and the ferries

Santa Caterina del Sasso

3 Rocca di Angera, Lake Maggiore

This 8th-century Lombard fortress dominates Angera's headland. Expanded in the late 13th century by the Visconti of Milan, it later became the seat of its own county, and in 1449 passed to the Borromeo clan. Today the glowering fortress preserves delicate medieval frescoes and a Doll Museum *(see also p99).*

4 Bellagio, Lake Como

Perhaps the loveliest town on any of the lakes has it all: a harbourside arcade of cafés, sumptuous gardens surrounding stately villas, steep medieval alleys, and hotels and shops in all price ranges. The Romanesque church of San Giacomo has a 12th-century pulpit with reliefs of the Evangelists *(see also pp108 & 110).*

5 Como's Duomo, Lake Como

The exterior of Como's cathedral, begun in the late 14th century, is a festival of statues and bas-reliefs. Inside are Renaissance altar-pieces and tapestries *(see p107)*.

6 Villa Carlotta, Lake Como

Owing its beauty and fame to three owners, the villa itself was begun in 1643 for Giorgio Clerici. In 1801 it passed to lawyer Gian Battista

Quiet alley in Varenna

Sommariva, and he filled it with Neo-Classical sculptures and Romantic paintings. The former include *Palamede* by Canova and *Cupid and Psyche* by his student Tadolini; the latter a famed *Last Kiss of Romeo and Juliet* by Francesco Hayez, master of stolen-kiss scenes. In 1847 it passed to the Prussian Princess Carlotta, who lent it her name while her husband, Prince Giorgio di Sassonia-Meiningen, furnished it in Empire style. He also created the magnificent botanical gardens *(see pp44 & 108)*.

7 Varenna, Lake Como

Varenna is less touristy than Bellagio and almost as rewarding. It has a waterfront promenade, two small churches with medieval frescoes on the main square, two villas-with-gardens to wander, and the half-ruined Castello di Vezio high above town. Just south of Varenna, the Fiumelatte gushes from the cliff face down about 250 m (800 ft) into the lake, making it the shortest river in Italy. Oddly, it flows only from March to October *(see also pp108–9 & 110)*.

8 Il Vittoriale, Lake Garda

An over-the-top Art Nouveau overhaul of this villa owned by the flamboyant poet, adventurer and national hero Gabriele d'Annunzio was financed by none other than Mussolini himself – basically as a bribe to silence d'Annunzio's criticism of the fascist government *(see also pp45 & 118)*.

9 Sirmione, Lake Garda

Jutting into the lake from the southern shore is a skinny peninsula. At its tip sits the postcard-perfect town of Sirmione, guarded by a striking castle complete with moat and drawbridge. It's a popular resort, with plenty of hotels and shopping, but also some fine little churches and the ruins of a Roman villa at the promontory's very tip *(see pp117 & 120)*.

10 Giardino Botanico Hruska, Lake Garda

Arturo Hruska, Swiss dentist to Europe's royalty in the early and mid-20th century, laid out these sumptuous botanical gardens between 1940 and 1971 *(see pp45 & 118)*.

A steep lane in picturesque Bellagio

Left **Borromeo Palace** Centre **Gardens, Villa Carlotta** Right **Terrace, Villa Monastero**

🔟 Villas and Gardens

1 Borromeo Palace, Lake Maggiore

The Borromeo family's 1670 *palazzo* on the lushly landscaped Isola Bella is an incomparable glimpse into the lifestyle of the wealthiest of Lombard families (see p22).

2 Villa Taranto, Lake Maggiore

The villa at Verbania *(see p100)*, built in 1875 by Scotsman Neil MacEacharn, is closed to the public, but you can wander the English-landscaped gardens filled with exotic plants. Rare species include the world's largest water lily at 2 m (6 ft) across and the towering Metasequoia, which was believed extinct for 200 million years until found in China in 1941.
◈ *Via Vittorio Veneto, Pallanza, Verbania • Map A2 • 0323-556-667 • www.villa taranto.it • 8:30am–7:30pm daily; last entry 6:30pm • Closed Nov–end Mar • Adm*

3 Villa Carlotta, Lake Como

Lake Como is famous for its extravagant villas, but while some gardens are open, few of the buildings themselves can be visited. At Villa Carlotta, however,

Borromeo Palace and Lake Maggiore

Fountain, Villa Taranto

you can visit both the late Baroque villa filled with Neo-Classical statues and Romantic paintings, and the extensive, lush gardens *(see pp43 & 108)*.

4 Villa Serbelloni, Lake Como

The villa's private gardens cover the entire tip of the Bellagio promontory. The tours stick mainly to the paths, overlooking Italianate, English-style and Mediterranean sections. Stendhal described the vista from the top as "sublime and enchanting" – indeed, it's the only spot from which you can see down all three arms of Lake Como simultaneously *(see p108)*.

5 Villa Melzi, Lake Como

Francesco Melzi, the Vice-President of Napoleon's Cisalpine Republic, had this Neo-Classical villa built on Bellagio's southern edge. The villa is off-limits, but you can wander the gardens to the water's edge, visit a small museum (Etruscan, Egyptian and Roman artifacts) and see a mock Moorish temple that inspired a pair of Liszt piano concertos, written during the composer's stay here *(see p108)*.

6 Villa Monastero, Lake Como

The original structure was not really a monastery, but a Cistercian convent founded in 1208. It was disbanded by Charles Borromeo in the 16th century after he heard lascivious stories about its nuns. After centuries

Entrance, Villa Cipressi

as a noble villa, it's now owned by a science research centre. You can visit a terrace of palms, cypresses, magnolias and roses, and a greenhouse of citrus trees *(see p108)*.

7 Villa Balbianello, Lake Como

Department store mogul and explorer Guido Monzino gave this 1784 villa and its gorgeous gardens to FAI (the Italian National Trust) in 1988. A museum inside chronicles his adventures from Mount Everest to the North Pole. The property pole-vaulted to the front of famous Como sights after appearing in *Star Wars: Episode II* *(see pp51 & 107)*.

8 Villa Cipressi, Lake Como

Fancy spending the night at one of Lake Como's gorgeous villas? The Cipressi is now a hotel, and guests can wander its cypress-shaded gardens, blooming with wisteria, for free *(see pp109 & 113)*.

9 Il Vittoriale, Lake Garda

This kitschy Art Nouveau villa was created by poet and adventurer Gabriele d'Annunzio, a flamboyant man who once flew a biplane over Vienna in 1918 to prove an invasion was possible, and in 1919 used private troops to take over a border town ceded to Yugoslavia, earning himself acclaim as a national hero and the enmity of those in power. The villa represents his life, loves and philosophy, which are cheerfully explained by guides. The famous plane is preserved in an outbuilding *(see p118)*.

10 Giardino Botanico Hruska, Lake Garda

Swiss dentist and naturalist Arturo Hruska may have had only a single hectare of lake property, but over 30 years he managed to turn it into a microcosm of Dolomite and Alpine flora. Since 1989, Austrian multimedia artist André Heller has kept it open it to the public *(see p118)*.

Villa Balbianello

Left **Pavia** Right **Vigevano**

Small Towns and Villages

1 Sabbioneta
An entire town planned between 1556 and 1591 to Renaissance ideals, Sabbioneta is the legacy of Vespasiano Gonzaga Borromeo, who, bereft of heirs, put his energies into a complex of palaces and a theatre *(see p127)*.

Crema

2 Crema
Though originally a fiercely loyal satellite of Milan, Crema's formative period was under the Venetians (1454–1797). It's a tidy town of white and pink marble façades, a delightful Duomo and a civic museum that includes scores by composer Francesco Cavalli.
🔊 *Map E5 • Tourist info: Via dei Racchetti 8 • 0373-81-020 • www.prolococrema.it*

3 Lodi
Built in 1158 after Barbarossa *(see p32)* razed the original town 5 km (3 miles) to the west, Lodi is celebrated for its Duomo and

octagonal church of the Incoronata. The latter is slathered with frescoes, gilded stuccoes and fine paintings by Il Bergognone.
🔊 *Map D5 • Tourist info: Piazza Broletto 4 • 0371-421-391 • www.turismo. provincia.lodi.it*

4 Pavia
The capital of northern Italy in the Dark Ages is now lost in Milan's suburban sprawl but retains its historic centre. In addition to the glorious Certosa *(see pp24–5)*, other important churches include San Pietro in Ciel d'Oro and San Michele, both full of Romanesque carvings, and the Duomo, whose architects included Bramante and Leonardo. Pavia also boasts a Renaissance bridge and 14th-century castle with paintings by Antonella da Messina, Correggio, Bellini, Luini and Tiepolo. 🔊 *Map C6 • Tourist info: Via Fabio Filzi 2 • 0382-597-001 • www.turismo.provincia.pv.it*

Renaissance bridge, Pavia

Bormio

5 Vigevano
Lodovico "Il Moro" Sforza *(see p33)* was born in the castle that dominates this town of silk and shoe factories. The arcaded Piazza Ducale was designed by Bramante; the Baroque Duomo was built in 1680. ◈ *Map B5*
• *www.vigevano.org*

6 Castiglione Olona
In the 14th century Cardinal Branda Castiglione fell in love with the new Gothic painting style he saw in Florence and was determined to import it to his hometown. The aging painter Masolino did some of his best works in the cardinal's palace and the Chiesa della Collegiata. The Chiesa della Villa nearby is a Brunelleschian church with colossal saints flanking the entrance. ◈ *Map B3 • Tourist info: Piazza Garibaldi 4 • 0331-858-048*

7 Civate
The main town on little Lake Annone was a medieval stop for pilgrims visiting its 8th-century abbey, which was said to house a set of Saint Peter's Keys to Heaven (long-vanished). In the hills above town is the stunning Romanesque retreat of San Pietro al Monte *(see p110)*.

8 Chiavenna
This town in the Alpine valley is littered with *crotti* – caverns used to cure meats and cheeses – many of which have been converted into *osterie*. An old stone quarry above town is home to a botanical park; and the Parco Marmitte dei Giganti contains prehistoric carvings. ◈ *Tourist info: Corso V Emanuele II 2 • 0343-363-84 • www.valchiavenna.com/chiavenna*

9 Val Calmonica Villages
The villages of Capo di Ponte and Nadro di Ceto are the best access points for the prehistoric rock carvings found in the valley north of Lake Iseo. The images are at least 3,000 years old and include hunting scenes. ◈ *Tourist info: Via S Briscoli 42, Capo di Ponte • 0364-42-080 • www.invallecamonica.it*

10 Bormio
This year-round skiing village high in the Valtellina is equal parts high-class resort and medieval village. It's also a gateway to a park of glaciers, peaks, trails and gorgeous Alpine vistas. ◈ *Tourist info: Via Roma 131b • 0342-903-300 • www.valtellina.it*

Left **St Luke Polyptych by Mantegna** Centre **Study by Leonardo** Right **A portrait of Caravaggio**

Artists Working in Lombardy

1 Andrea Mantegna (1431–1506)

Mantegna's classical mode of High Renaissance painting differed from but was as ethereally beautiful as that of his brother-in-law Giovanni Bellini. In 1460 he became court painter to the Gonzagas of Mantova, where he left masterful frescoes on the walls of the Palazzo Ducale *(see p28)*. Milan's Pinacoteca di Brera houses his remarkably foreshortened *Dead Christ (see p12)*.

Self-portrait by Leonardo da Vinci

2 Bramante (1444–1514)

The great architect of the High Renaissance travelled from Urbino to Florence, then Milan and Rome, leaving churches in his wake (and doing a stint as chief architect of St Peter's in Rome). He favoured geometric designs and smooth walls, with architectural lines picked out in dark stone.

3 Leonardo da Vinci (1452–1519)

The ultimate Renaissance Man was a genius painter, inventor and scientist. His *sfumato* technique of blurring outlines and progressively hazing distances lent his works tremendous illusory depth. His inventions – including helicopters, machine guns and water systems – were centuries ahead of their time but mostly confined to sketches, though working models have now been built at Milan's technical museum. *(See pp8–9, 40 & 93.)*

4 Bernardino Luini (1475–1532)

This apprentice of Leonardo was so taken with his master's talents that he spent his life churning out paintings in the Leonardo style without ever really developing one of his own.

5 Il Bergognone (1480–1523)

With the Renaissance raging all around him, Il Bergognone remained firmly a late Gothic painter, cranking out lovely but staid devotional paintings rooted in the style of his Milanese predecessor Vincenzo Foppa.

Self-portrait by Futurist Umberto Boccioni

6 Giulio Romano (1499–1546)

Raphael's protégé helped finish his master's commissions after his death, but his fame as a frescoist was soon eclipsed by his architectural technique. Both came to the attention of the Gonzagas in Mantova, who commissioned from him the Palazzo Te *(see p29)* and other buildings. Only failing health kept him from returning to Rome to become chief architect of St Peter's.

7 Giuseppe Arcimboldo (1527–93)

This Milanese Mannerist was a gimmick artist, but very good at it. He churned out allegorical "portraits" that are actually collages: of flowers, fruit, fish, weapons, animals or even flames.

8 Caravaggio (1571–1609/10)

The Baroque master, who influenced an entire generation, used peasant models and a technique of heavy chiaroscuro, playing harsh light off deep black shadows to create dramatic scenes with brilliant realism.

9 Francesco Hayez (1707–76)

Born in Venice, Hayez moved to Rome – where he mixed with Ingres and Canova – then Milan, balancing his painting between the Romantic and Neo-Classical ideals of the age. He became director of the Pinacoteca di Brera.

10 Umberto Boccioni (1882–1916)

This leading Futurist was born in the south but soon moved to Milan. His failed journalism career served him in writing treatises on Futurism, while his paintings and sculptures were among the most admired of his era.

Top 10 Artistic Eras in Lombardy

1 Ancient
From prehistoric rock etchings dating back to the 12th century BC to sophisticated Roman villas of the 5th century AD.

2 Lombard
Lombard buildings from the 5th to 10th centuries feature triangular façades, blind arcades and ribbed vaulting.

3 Romanesque
A simple style of architecture in the 11th and 12th centuries defined by rounded arches and crude, expressive carvings.

4 Gothic
Pointed arches and flying buttresses allowed ceilings to soar in the 13th and 14th centuries. Painting became more expressive and realistic.

5 Renaissance
Classical architecture and elegant painting, with delicate colours and new techniques such as perspective (15th–16th centuries).

6 Baroque
The Renaissance but with profuse décor; big in the 17th century, then spiralled into overwrought Rococo in the 18th.

7 Neo-Classical
Late 18th to early 19th-century quest for the soul of the ancients; austere in style.

8 Romantic
A 19th-century return to the Gothic age and overwrought décor.

9 Liberty
The Italian Art Nouveau of the early 20th century delighted in asymmetrical organic curves.

10 Futurist
Italy's Cubism was obsessed with the modern world of the early 20th century.

Left **Film version of** *I Promessi Sposi* Right **Antonioni's** *La Notte*

🔟 Books and Films Set in Lombardy

1 I Promessi Sposi (The Betrothed)

Written in the 1800s, Alessandro Manzoni's novel is a window into Lombard life in the 1600s, set in Milan and Manzoni's Lake Como hometown of Lecco during Spanish rule. It is required reading for all Italian schoolchildren and has been translated into many languages.

2 A Farewell to Arms

Ernest Hemingway's World War I novel (written in 1929) tells the story of an American soldier wounded while fighting for the Italian army. He convalesces in a Milan hospital, and, after inadvertently deserting while escaping the Germans, reunites with his love in Stresa on Lake Maggiore. They stay at the

Rock Hudson and Jennifer Jones in the 1957 film of *A Farewell to Arms*

Des Iles Borromées hotel (where Hemingway himself often stayed) before fleeing by boat across to Swiss Locarno.

3 Twilight in Italy

The first place D H Lawrence and his lover Frieda settled during their European peregrinations was the shores of Lake Garda, during the winter of 1912–13. In 1916 he compiled his notes on those happy first months spent in Italy and wrote this travelogue.

4 A Month by the Lake

It's 1937, and a group of stodgy society Brits and bored Yanks loosen their mores and inhibitions on the shores of Lake Como. Vanessa Redgrave and Uma Thurman head up the cast of this 1995 film by John Irvin. You can visit its setting, the Villa Balbianello *(see p45)*.

5 Miracle in Milan

Vittorio de Sica's 1951 fable of a magical dove that grants wishes to the inhabitants of a Milan slum uses an early version of "special effects", bridging the popular Neo-Realistic style of Italy's post-war cinema with the era of magical realism in film-making that Fellini would make famous.

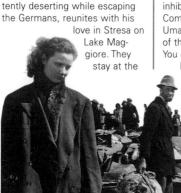

Vittorio de Sica's *Miracle in Milan*

6 A Traveller in Italy
H V Morton, who in his youth gained fame scooping the story of Tutankhamun's tomb discovery in the 1920s, became one of the 20th-century's best, if little-known, travel writers. His 1950s journey through Italy is an erudite combination of travelogue, history and wonderful prose, all of it surprisingly undated.

7 La Notte
Film director Michelangelo Antonioni takes the slow death of affection between a couple, masterfully played by Marcello Mastroianni and Jeanne Moreau, and sets it against a backdrop of rapidly industralizing Milan in 1960.

8 Theorem
Pier Paolo Pasolini's usual mix of sex, homosexuality and a communist critique on the emptiness of bourgeois life defines this 1968 film. Handsome stranger Terrence Stamp raises the libidos of a middle-class Milanese family, then further stirs up their lives by disappearing.

9 The Spider's Strategem
Before gaining international fame, Bernardo Bertolucci made this 1969 story of a dysfunctional family haunted by the fascist past. He set this psychological drama in the quirky town of Sabbioneta.

10 Star Wars Episode II
George Lucas knew that even his vaunted digital special effects couldn't hold a candle to the extraterrestrial beauty of Lake Como, which, with very little touching-up, filled in for Naboo's lake district in the fifth Star Wars instalment, *Attack of the Clones* (2002). Beautiful Villa Balbianello *(see p45)* is again a backdrop for romantic scenes.

Top 10 La Scala Premieres

1 L'Europa Riconosciuta (1778)
Salieri's bellicose but light-hearted opera opened La Scala on 3 August 1778.

2 La Pietra del Paragone (1812)
Rossini's work signalled La Scala's shift from comic opera and Neo-Classical works to Romantic melodrama.

3 Chiara e Serafina (1822)
The first of many fun-loving Donizetti premieres.

4 Norma (1831)
Of Bellini's three La Scala premieres, the most famous is *Norma*, a Druid-Roman love triangle that ends badly.

5 Nabucco (1842)
Verdi would become La Scala's greatest home-grown composer, but he suffered two flops before this hit.

6 Mefistofele (1868)
Boito's first great success led to a collaboration with Verdi that produced *Otello* in 1887 and *Falstaff* in 1893.

7 Aïda (1872)
After a long absence from La Scala, Verdi offered this Egyptian melodrama.

8 Madame Butterfly (1904)
Puccini's tale of enduring love between a Japanese geisha and an American soldier.

9 Turandot (1926)
Puccini struck lucky again with exotic Asian fare – and, for once, a happy(ish) ending.

10 The Rake's Progress (1951)
Under Toscanini's direction, La Scala started opening up to foreign works, including this Stravinsky classic.

Left **Sagra del Carroccio** Right **Festa dei Navigli**

Festivals and Events

1 Carnival

Carnevale in Milan is a combination of religious pomp, fancy-dress parade and Bacchanalian bash. Whereas carnivals elsewhere in the world – everywhere from Rio to Venice – end on Martedì Grasso ("Fat Tuesday"), Archbishop St Ambrose decreed that in Milan the party should go on until the following Saturday. No wonder they made him a saint. ◈ *Feb/Mar (ends the first Sat of Lent)* • *Info: 02-7252-4301*

2 Modamilano

Milan's most important holiday is a biannual fashion trade fair. Even if you're not here for the fashion shows, MODIT will affect your stay: hotels are booked well in advance. Plan (and pack) accordingly. ◈ *Approx 1 week, early Mar & early Oct* • *Info: Viale Sarca 223* • *02-643-3669* • *www.momimodamilano.it*

Modamilano

3 Sagra del Carroccio

Two years after the Lombard League trounced Barbarossa in 1176 *(see p32)*, the town of Legnano began celebrating the victory. Over 800 yeas later they're still at it, putting on a display of pageantry that ends with a horse race between the town's eight *contrade* (districts). ◈ *Last Sun in May* • *Info: Comitato Sagra del Carroccio* • *Piazza S Magno* • *0331-471-258*

4 Festa dei Navigli

Milan's trendy Navigli canal district celebrates the start of summer on the first Sunday in June by bursting into a street fair with artisan stalls and live music. ◈ *First Sun in Jun*

5 Ferragosto

August 15, the Feast of the Assumption, is the day most Italians head to the beach or lakes for a two-week holiday, and life in the city comes to a halt. Mantua has a 15 August celebration of street artists, but Milan virtually shuts down. Only the restaurants and bars of the Navigli stay open. ◈ *15–31 Aug*

6 Settimane Musicali, Stresa

Lake Maggiore's gateway to the Borromean Islands *(see p99)* hosts five musical weeks of concerts in venues throughout town and up and down the lake shores. ◈ *Late Aug–end Sep* • *Info: Via Carducci 38* • *0323-31-095* • *www.settimanemusicali.net*

7 Grand Prix, Monza

The biggest Formula One race of the year takes place in mid-September. At other times, you can still watch macho men driving cars at mind-boggling speeds from April through to October. ◈ *Grand Prix: 2nd weekend in Sep* • *Info: Via Vedano 5* • *039-24-821* • *www.monzanet.it*

8 Stringed Instruments Festivals, Cremona

The home of Amati and Stradivarius celebrates luthiers and musicians in a series of festivals. An annual exhibition of instruments is accompanied by related contests *(see also pp35 & 127)*. ✦ *October • Info: Ente Triennale degli Strumenti ad Arco, Corso Matteotti 17 • 0372-21-454 • www.entetriennale.com*

9 Oh Bej! Oh Bej!, Milan

Milan celebrates its patron saint with a street fair surrounding Piazza Sant'Ambrogio. The name is said to have come from the delighted squeals of children who, upon beholding such a marvellous fair, once cried in Milanese dialect "Oh, how pretty! Oh, how pretty!" ✦ *5–8 Dec • Info: Piazza Sant'Ambrogio, Milan • 02-7252-4301*

10 Opera Season

La Scala *(see p74)* is the most important opera house in the world, and if you ever doubted opera was art, a night at its 18th-century home will help you transcend all doubt. The season opens on 7 December – the feast day of Milan's patron saint, Ambrose – and is a momentous occasion in the Milanese social calendar. ✦ *Info: 02-7200-3744 • tickets: 02-860-775 • www.teatroallascala.org*

Oh Bej! Oh Bej! street fair

Spectator Sports and Sporting Activities

1 Football (Soccer)

Lombardy boasts four Serie A teams, two of them in Milan *(see pp62–3)*. San Siro stadium is the main venue *(see p88)*.

2 Car Racing

The track at Monza, one of Europe's best, hosts the Italian Grand Prix in September (entry 7 opposite).

3 Horse Racing

Milan's Ippodromo *(see p88)* is the place to go for a flutter at the races.

4 Windsurfing

Stiff winds at the northern ends of the lakes make for some of the best lake wind-surfing in Western Europe.

5 Cycling

Whether speeding down the Mincio Valley, mountain-biking, or ambling along the lakeside roads, Lombardy is great on two wheels.

6 Sailing

The same breezes that fuel windsurfers are enjoyed by sailors, especially on Lakes Garda, Como and Iseo.

7 Horse Riding

The hills and valleys around Lake Maggiore provide the best terrain for saddling up *(see also p111)*.

8 Hiking

Take a bracing trek into the hills above the lakes.

9 Golf

The luxury hotels of the lakes have all invested in designer golf courses *(see also pp111 & 121)*.

10 Skiing

In their northern reaches the lakes are bound by Italian pre-Alps that extend the resorts' seasons year-round.

Following pages **Lake Maggiore's Isola Bella**

Left **Versace shop front** Centre **Antiques, Via Montenapoleone** Right **Moschino, Via della Spiga**

🔟 Shopping Meccas in Milan

1 Via Manzoni

This broad boulevard became an epicentre of Milanese fashion when Giorgio Armani opened his gargantuan superstore here in 2000 *(see p77)*. On Manzoni there's everything from the Roman fashions of Davide Cenci (No. 7) to the check-me-out jewellery of Donatella Pellini (No. 20). ✎ *Map M2–3*

2 Galleria Vittorio Emanuele II

Milan's glorious 19th-century shopping mall *(see p74)*, though small, manages to host a little of everything. You'll find both the pinnacle of class (Prada) and the joys of mass-market culture (a Ricordi/Feltrinelli superstore of CDs and books). For a shopping break, visit the home-grown bastion of *la dolce vita* that is Zucca in Galleria *(see p80)*. ✎ *Map M3*

Prada, Via Montenapoleone

3 Corso Vittorio Emanuele II

This thoroughly modernized pedestrian street at the back of the Duomo is lined with arcades and some of the hippest shops in central Milan. Techno beats throb from windows displaying international cutting-edge chic for young fashionistas. ✎ *Map M4–N3*

4 Via P Verri

Fashion-conscious men should head for Via P Verri, where they'll find the menswear outlet of Zegna (No. 3, *see p77*), supplier of sharp suits and sartorial weekend attire. Two doors along at No. 1 is a wonderful little boutique for Canali's suits. ✎ *Map M–N3*

5 Via Montenapoleone

Rodeo Drive, Fifth Avenue, rue du Faubourg-St-Honoré...

Galleria Vittorio Emanuele II

none can claim the hometown boutiques of Prada, Armani, Versace and more. Via Montenapoleone – "Montenapo" to its friends – is the main artery of Milan's Quadrilatero d'Oro, a "Golden Rectangle" of streets where the top international

Via della Spiga

names in high fashion congregate alongside the best antiques and art dealers and a few classy cafés. ⊗ *Map M2–N3*

6 Via Borgospesso
In the Quadrilatero d'Oro, this street has the highest concentration of art and antique shops, from lacquered 17th-century Venetian boxes at Silva (No. 12) to a bit of everything at Silbernagl *(see p79)*. ⊗ *Map M–N2*

7 Via della Spiga
For sheer shopping volume head to Via della Spiga, which has more worthy shops than any other street in all of Milan. Here's just a sample of the well-known names on offer here: Dolce e Gabbana (2, 26), Bottega Veneta (5), Gherardini (8), Tiffany & Co. (19a), Gaultier (20), Krizia (23), Roberto Cavalli (42) and Sermoneta Gloves (46). ⊗ *Map N2*

8 Corso Buenos Aires
This long road is where your average Milanese heads to shop, offering more than 350 shops in no particular order. You'll find everything from handmade men's dress shirts and Richard Ginori china to bootleg records. ⊗ *Map P1*

9 Via San Gregorio
The grid of streets southeast of Milan's Stazione Centrale train station is Milan's best-kept shopping secret. Over 100 clothing warehouses and distributors pepper Via San Gregorio, Via Boscovich, Via C Tenca and others, offering cut-price goods.

10 Milan's Markets
The big Milan market is Saturday's Fiera di Senigallia along the Darsena canal. Milan's Sunday flea market surrounds the San Donato metro stop in the south. Local markets are on Via San Marco (Mondays), Via Benedetto Marcello (northeast of the Giardini Pubblici) on Tuesdays, and Viale Papiniano in the Navigli (Saturdays). Markets tend to shut by 1pm, except on Saturday. ⊗ *Maps J–K6 (Darsena canal), M1 (Via San Marco), J5 (Papiniano)*

Left **English-language bookshop** Centre **Jewellery display, Via della Spiga** Right **Objets d'art**

Things to Buy

1 Designer Clothes
Milan, of course, is monumentally important to the world of fashion. Every important fashion label, whether local or based in Paris, New York or Florence, maintains a boutique in Milan. For those whose tastes outstrip their budgets, Milan is also home to some excellent stock shops and discount outlets.

2 Shoes
Italian shoes range from the practical to the gorgeous and outrageous. Some will last you a lifetime; some are just for very special occasions. All the famous labels offer lines of shoes, but you'd do best to seek out the specialists, whether it be a haute-couture work of art at Ferragamo *(see p78)*, a mass-produced Italian brand name or a designer bargain from Rufus *(see p89)*.

3 Handbags
Swoon over the designs from Prada and Bottega Veneta, or the slightly less pricey Coccinelle. Or, plump for one of the many well made, non-label leather bags, still in great Italian style.

4 Design Objects
Italian industrial designers are maestros at turning everyday objects such as kettles, lighting systems and juicers into works

Prada shoes and bags

of art. The often whimsical, usually beautiful and always ergonomically sound results are on sale throughout Italy, or you can go right to the source on Lake Orta. Here, an artisan tradition gave rise in the late 19th century to firms such as Alessi, Bialetti and Lagostina.

5 Linens
Bassetti and Frette offer affordable, stylish linens. The haute couture of sheets and tablecloths is represented by Pratesi and, at the pinnacle, Jerusum, which provided the lace-edged linens for Italy's royal family in the 19th century.

6 Silk
Como has long been Italy's chief purveyor of finely spun silk fabrics. The Milanese maestros of haute couture come to Como to finger the fabrics that will soon be draped across a supermodel's shoulders. These same sought-after silks are available to the public in factory warehouses around Como and in shops across Lombardy.

7 Art and Antiques
Milan's art dealers offer a rich collection of lesser-known Byzantine and Baroque works and a plethora of 19th-century oils and other relatively affordable works of art. You'll find an

Italy's celebration of la dolce vita, *the art of living well, is nowhere more apparent than in its range of beautiful things to buy* embarrassment of 18th-century Venetian chairs, country-style hardwood dressers and Empire-style clocks cluttering the *antichità* shops.

8 Wine
Lombard wines are generally excellent *(see p67)*. Furthermore, the lakes border both the Veneto – home to Valpolicella, Pinot Grigio and Soave – and Piemonte, where the mighty Barolo, Barbera and Barbaresco reds are crafted.

9 Books
A catalogue of Milanese galleries, a glossy tome of lake scenes or a translation of local literary classic *I Promessi Sposi* *(see p50)* might be a more treasured souvenir than a sheaf of postcards or trinkets.

10 Jewellery
Though it's not a top European capital of baubles and precious gems, Milan's jewellers hold their own. Seek out the bold creations of Donatella Pellini or the cutting-edge minimalism of Xenia. For something more classic, try Gobbi 1842 and especially Mario Buccellati, a firm that since 1919 has produced exquisite jewellery, elegant tableware and renowned silver *objets d'art*.

Antique glassware, Via Montenapoleone

Top 10 Fashion Houses and Gurus

1 Armani
Italy's top fashion guru is the master of smart clothes that, for a price tag with far too many zeroes, can help anyone look like a model.

2 Versace
Made "violently elegant" designs popular and costumed many La Scala productions in the 1980s.

3 Prada
The most chillingly expensive of Milan designers, Prada breathed new life into relaxed minimalism with the help of a small red stripe.

4 Mila Schön
A giant of fashion who pioneered the double-face fabric in the 1960s.

5 Krizia
Ever an eclectic designer, Mariuccia "Krizia" Mandelli has been flouting trends and winning awards since 1954.

6 Ermenegildo Zegna
Fourth-generation, environmentally-aware firm that uses the finest cashmere, merino and mohair in its fabrics.

7 Moschino
An *enfant terrible* of Milan's fashion scene since 1983.

8 Missoni
This husband-wife team has charmed the fashion world since 1953 with its multi-coloured, zigzag knitwear.

9 Trussardi
Founded by a Bergamasco glove-maker in 1910, Trussardi produces classic cuts and gorgeous leather accessories.

10 Ferré
His recent lines are aimed at the youth market (Ferré Jeans) and people of a larger build (Ferré Forma).

Left **Auditorium di Milano** Right **Rolling Stone**

Entertainment Venues in Milan

1 La Scala
This is Milan's – indeed, one of the world's – top opera companies, where Verdi was once house composer, Callas formerly graced the stage and costumes are designed by top fashion artistes. Performances have now returned to this gloriously restored 18th-century theatre after three years at the purpose-built Teatro degli Arcimboldi *(see p74)*.

2 Scimmie
Part bar, part restaurant, part pizzeria and part jazz club that doesn't limit itself to jazz. In summer, the party spills out onto a barge moored opposite. Since 1971, "Monkeys" has been shaking up the Navigli nightlife scene with live music daily until 3am *(see p96)*.

3 Auditorium di Milano
The "Giuseppe Verdi" Symphony Orchestra of Milan has since 1999 played in this re-invented 1930s' cinema, which stood derelict for decades after World War II. Riccardo Chailly conducts concerts from late September to May. ✵ *Via S Gottardo 42 • www.orchestrasinfonica. milano.it • Concerts: 8:30pm Thu & Fri, 4pm Sun; chamber music: 11am Sun; Kids' musical programme: 3:30pm Sat*

4 Limelight
This is high-tech nightclubbing, with TV screens, internet feeds, concerts broadcast live and a magnetic card that keeps track of your tab (you pay when you leave). The music ranges from modern pop and hip-hop to 1960s and 70s revival – the owners are a group of Serie A footballers who are often seen here when not on the field *(see p96)*. ✵ *Via Castelbarco 11*

5 Magazzini Generali
Cavernous Magazzini Generali is a little bit of everything. It has a stage and auditorium that seats 1,000 for live acts, it can become a huge disco, it has a gallery for exhibitions, and it fits in live poetry readings and more besides. ✵ *Via Pietrasanta 14 • 02-5521-1313*

6 Plastic
If you feel it just ain't a club unless there's bouncers and

La Scala

Magazzini Generali

velvet ropes keeping the less-than-perfect at bay, then Plastic is the spot for you. Inside, there's a mix of techno, house and jungle – background to the pick-up scene for all tastes (Thursday is officially gay/lesbian night). There's also a laid-back billiards room, with jukebox favourites.
◈ Viale Umbria 120 • 02-733-996

Rolling Stone
7 Rolling Stone is as classic as the band after which it is named; a no-excuses, party-hard, rock-music discotheque filling a cavernous ex-cinema with huge crowds drawn to hear the best live rock acts of any venue in town. We're talking everything from Iron Maiden to Van Morrison, Nick Cave to Oasis. Weekends – when there are no international rock stars on the bill – the sound system is turned over to Milan's top DJs, and the crowd gets a chance to throw down some moves on the floor (see p96).

Boulevard Café
8 This arty Brera hold-out of bohemianism squeezes a tiny stage and an enthusiastic

crowd into a narrow space to enjoy live music. It's as popular as it is small; don't expect to get a table, or be able to hear the person next to you (see p90).

Hollywood
9 This stalwart from the 1980s still offers you the best chance in all of Milan to spot a genuine international supermodel. Though a perfectly standard discotheque from 1986, glitzy Hollywood continues to draw the most beautiful people in town, so dress to impress (see p90).

Tunnel
10 Tunnel is actually a warehouse squirrelled away under the arches on the back side of the main railway station (Stazione Centrale). This is the place to catch the next big thing in Italian, and sometimes even international, alternative rock acts and top DJs (see p90).

Left **Cycling in Mantova** Right **Gardaland theme park**

Attractions for Children

1 Exploring Milan's Duomo
Milan's cathedral is a Gothic wonderland of flying buttresses, soaring pinnacles, saintly statues, spiral staircases and hideous gargoyles – fun to explore for kids aged 5 to 95 *(see pp10–11)*.

2 The Best Science Museum in Italy
Milan's Museo Nazionale della Scienza e delle Tecnica has the usual impressive collection of a major science museum – historic cars, TV sets, steam engines, a planetarium and (in the Naval Museum upstairs) thousands of model ships – and it also has Leonardo. The Renaissance genius "invented" (at least on paper) everything from helicopters to labour-saving mechanical devices. Full-scale models help bring his visions to life and may just help pique a youngster's interest in the whole Renaissance thing *(see p93)*.

3 Puppet Shows
Italy's rich tradition of puppet shows, from Sicily's epic tales of Saracen warriors and Charlemagne's knights to Naples' slapstick Pulcinella (Punch and Judy) shows, has almost died out. Thankfully, here and there master puppeteers such as Cosetta and Gianni Colla at Milan's Teatro delle Marionette keep the tradition alive and update the stories to appeal to a modern audience.

Gelato (ice cream)

⊗ Teatro delle Marionette, Via Tullio Ostilio 1, Milan • 02-468-260 for show times

4 Milan's Toy Museum
The Museo del Giocattolo e del Bambino in Milan traces the history of play from the 18th century to today in display cases built at a child's-eye level. The exhibits are protected behind glass, but there is a small playroom for some hands-on fun. ⊗ Via R Pitteri 56, Milan; www.museodelgiocattolo.it • 9:30am–4pm Mon–Fri, 9:30am–12:30pm, 3–6pm Sat, Sun & hols • Adm

5 Gelato Breaks
Italy's *gelato* puts all other ice creams in the world to shame. There are dozens of classic parlours around Milan, including Rachelli (Via Hugo 4), Bastianello (Via Borgogna 5) and Grasso (Viale Doria 17). Elsewhere, be sure there's the sign *"produzione propria"*, indicating that it's homemade. The true litmus test is to look for natural colours: you want banana that's naturally (if unappetizingly) grey, not bright yellow.

6 Football for Young Fans
An emotion-packed *calcio* (football) match at Milan's striking San Siro stadium *(see p88)* is fun for sports fans of all ages. And with two Serie A teams calling Milan home – Inter and AC Milan – the chances of catching a top-flight match during the season are

excellent. Check out their websites for game schedules, or the Lega-Calcio website for information on Lombardy's other two Serie A squads, Como and Brescia. Alternatively, the Inter-Milan Museum (Gate 4, San Siro) comprises a visit to the stadium and the changing rooms. 🖰 www.inter.it • www.acmilan.com • www.lega-calcio.it

7 Gardaland
Italy's top theme park, by Lake Garda, is a far cry from Disneyland, but it does have roller coasters, a jungle safari and a thrilling water park (see p117). It's a place where older children can be dropped off for a day of fun while the parents drive off to explore those "boring villas and gardens" the kids are probably complaining about right now.

8 Windsurfing Lessons on Lake Garda
Garda is near perfect for all levels of surfers. There's enough wind to satisfy the experienced, but since the lake waters are relatively calm for most of the time, even novices can get out there and learn the techniques.

9 Lakeside Castles
You can relive the Middle Ages by exploring Lombardy's castles, scrambling up watchtowers and patrolling the ramparts

Windsurfing on Lake Garda

like a soldier of old. The Castello Sforzesco in Milan (see pp16–17) is mostly a museum, though regular tours take you up onto the battlements. Those on the lakes can be more atmospheric, some with intriguing museums, others romantically half in ruins. The best fortresses are at Varenna (see p110), and Arco, Malcésine and Sirmione (p117) by Lake Garda.

10 Cycling in Mantova
The city of Mantova is flat, virtually surrounded by lakes and plains that stretch up and down the Mincio River, all of it begging to be explored on two wheels. It's a welcome break from all the churches and museums that can numb even an avid art fan, and a chance to delve into the more physical side of Italian culture.

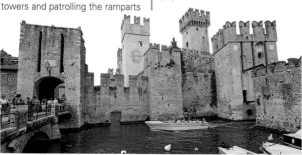

Rocca Scagliera at Sirmione, by Lake Garda

Left **Cova, Milan** Centre **Caffè del Tasso, Bergamo** Right **I Portici del Comune, Cremona**

🔟 Cafés and Wine Bars

1 Zucca (Caffè Miani), Milan

Caffè Zucca, Milan

Verdi and Toscanini would stop by after La Scala shows and King Umberto I declared that it served the best coffee in Milan. It even shows up in Boccioni's *Riot in the Galleria* (see p12). This café opened inside the Galleria Vittoria Emanuele (see p56) in 1868, though the Art Nouveau décor came a little later. Its prime location at the galleria entrance gives a great view of the Duomo façade (see p80).

2 Cova, Milan

The Faccioli family opened Cova near La Scala theatre in 1817 and, though it was later moved to Milan's prime shopping street, Via Montenapoleone, it has remained in the family – and continues to be café of choice for the city's elite – ever since. Its made-in-house pastries, chocolates and sandwiches are some of the most exquisite in town, and they brew up a mean cappuccino to boot. There's an elegant little tea room with refined service if all the window shopping has left you too tired to stand, but since this is still Italy, you're also welcome to just run in and toss back an espresso (see p80).

3 Sant'Ambroseus, Milan

Looking every inch the 1936 café, from its wood-panelling to its pink stucco decorations, Sant'Ambroseus is counted among the great temples of chocolate in Italy. Their speciality is the *ambrogiotti*: an indulgence of dark chocolate wrapped around an egg cream (see p80).

Cova, Milan

Pasticceria Marchesi, Milan

Corso Como 10, Milan
Run by former Vogue fashion
editor Carla Sozzani with the
same over-priced, excruciatingly
trendy verve that has made her
attached boutique such a popular
success, the café offers great
aperitivi and a chance to hobnob
with Milan's elite *(see p89)*.

Caffè Letterario, Milan
When Teresa D'Ambrosio
opened this place, she envisaged
the *fin de siècle* cafés where
artists met, writers scribbled away
at corner tables, professors spent
an hour or two poring over the
papers and political thinkers made
plans in hushed tones. And,
indeed, Milan's intelligentsia do
appear to have taken the bait and
placed themselves at appropriate
tables. ✆ *Via Solferino 27*

Bar Magenta, Milan
A lovely corner café that's
a cross between an Irish pub
and a Parisian Art Deco café,
with a zinc bar, high ceilings, free
newspapers and a decent list of
dishes along with coffee, beer,
cocktails and apéritifs *(see p90)*.

Pasticceria Marchesi, Milan
A wonderful old-fashioned
café and chocolatier happily
"discovered" by many a visitor

trekking out to see the *Last
Supper*. The décor hasn't
changed since 1824, the coffee
is quite good and the pastries
are favoured by Giorgio Armani
(see p90).

Vineria Cozzi, Bergamo
Don't let the over-busy
window decorations and trilling
recorded birdsong put you off –
Cozzi is the best spot in all of
Bergamo to while away an hour
or two with some wine and a
choice of cheeses, cured meats,
quiches and tortes *(see p128)*.

Caffè del Tasso, Bergamo
For over 500 years, the Tasso
has been Bergamo's meeting
spot for everyone from princes
to rebels. Garibaldi and his red
shirts met here in revolutionary
days; in fact, it was once such a
hotbed of discontent that a
decree (displayed on the wall)
was made in 1845 prohibiting
rebellious conversations here.
Now the only seditious senti-
ments are grumbles about the
price of a cappuccino *(see p128)*.

**I Portici del Comune,
Cremona**
You just can't get a better seat in
town than one at an outdoor
table set under a lofty medieval
arcade with the façade of Cremona's Duomo filling up your
panorama. The coffee is good
(not always a given), as are the
panini and *gelato (see p128)*.

Vineria Cozzi, Bergamo

Left **Place setting, Bellagio** Centre **Regional cheeses** Right **Fried slices of polenta**

Culinary Highlights of Lombardy

1 Cotoletta alla Milanese
For proof that the Lombards are Germanic at heart, look no further than Milan's archetypal dish, a breaded veal cutlet which is, essentially, *wienerschnitzel*.

2 Ossobuco
Succulent veal chops, cut across the shin bone, dredged in flour, lightly fried, then slow-cooked in wine and tomatoes with a bit of lemon-parsley-garlic *gremolata* tossed on top. Proper *ossobuco* is served on the bone (its very name means "bone-hole", though that sounds better in Italian): digging out the rich marrow is an integral part of enjoying the dish.

3 Polenta
Northern Italy's corn-meal side dish can be prepared in any form, from a soupy mush to a paste firm enough to slice and fry. It's often studded with mushrooms or some other delicacy.

4 Risotto alla Milanese
If you order risotto in Italy, you usually have to wait at least 20 minutes as the cook must constantly stir the round arborio rice until it reaches the optimum gooiness. It's time-consuming to make in small batches, so most restaurants will

Cotoletta alla milanese

prepare it only for two or more people. Milanese often tinge their risotto bright yellow with saffron, and may throw in seasonal vegetables. In Mantova they spice it up with sausage.

5 Tortelli di Zucca
Mantova specializes in this slightly sweet first course, stuffing pockets of fresh pasta with a rich pumpkin paste. It's customarily topped with a simple butter and sage sauce.

6 Strangolapreti
They're called "priest-stranglers" because these little balls of ricotta and spinach are deemed so rich they'd choke a poor prelate's simple palate. Usually served under a butter and parmesan glaze, though sometimes with tomato sauce.

7 Casoeûla
Somewhere between a soup, a stew and a main course, this mighty Milanese dish throws

Risotto with fish

Casoeûla

sausage and chunks of pork chops and rinds into a thick cabbage soup, with dollops of polenta on the side. It'll stick to your ribs (and clog your arteries).

8 Lake Fish
Several fish favourites are plucked daily from Lombardy's lakes. The best include *persico* (perch), *lavarello* (a whitefish), *trota* (trout), *luccio* (pike), *coregone* (another whitefish) and *tinca* (tench).

9 Cheeses
Lombardy is the land of Italy's smelly king of blue-veined cheeses, gorgonzola, and its lesser-known cousin taleggio (no mould, just strongly-odoured goodness). It's also home to grana padana, which is easily confused with parmesan. On the milder end of the scale are the popular bel paese and spreadable marscarpone.

10 Panettone
All across Italy at Christmas time people snap up boxes of this traditional Lombard cake, though locals enjoy it year-round. It is quite dry, and studded with fruit and candied peel.

Panettone

Top 10 Wines

1 Bardolino
The best-known wine is a light, balanced red from Lake Garda's Veneto shore.

2 Valtellina
This meaty red from the hills of Lake Como is powerful: one type is named "Inferno".

3 Franciacorta
South of Lake Iseo, Italy's only DOCG sparkling wine; try Saten. Also red (Cabernet-Merlot) and white (Chardonnay-Pinot) DOCs.

4 Lambrusco
Thick, dark, fizzy red from Mantova. Cheap but delicious; great with pizza.

5 Oltrepò Pavese
Also slightly fizzy, lighter and tangier than Lambrusco. The Garda region also produces familiar varietals.

6 Garda Bresciano
A collection of wines from the lower reaches of Lake Garda, including Gropello and the rounder Chiaretto from the Mincio valley.

7 San Martino della Battaglia
A tart white made from Tocai grapes of Friuli; there's also a dessert liqueur version.

8 Lugana
This balanced white is made from Trebbiano grapes on the southern shores of Lake Garda.

9 San Colombano
Milan's own red is chiefly significant for making the DOC level despite being grown on the outskirts of an industrial city.

10 Grappa
Italy's firewater is a *digestivo* ("digestive" liqueur) distilled from the leftovers of the grape-squeezing process.

Left **Cracco-Peck** Centre **Lake fish** Right **Barchetta interior**

🔟 Restaurants

1 Cracco-Peck, Milan

In 2000–2001, this bastion of fine Milanese cooking was completely overhauled and reopened under the guidance of Carlo Cracco, who once worked in Alain Ducasse's fabled Montecarlo restaurant. You will find wonderful classics here, including risotto or *cotoletta alla milanese* and ossobuco (see pp66–7). If the stratospheric prices make you cringe, know that just around the corner at Via Spadari 9 is plain old "Peck", one of the finest food emporia in Italy, where raw ingredients and prepared dishes can make up a glorious picnic (see also p81).

Joia

2 Il Teatro del Four Seasons, Milan

Milan's youngest deluxe hotel has surprised a jaded public by creating two superlative restaurants. The better of the two is the more refined basement eatery where chef Sergio Mei oversees creative Mediterranean dishes. The *degustazione* (tasting) menu is magnificent (see p81).

3 La Milanese, Milan

Classic Milanese cooking doesn't get much more fundamental, or much better, than this. Service is dour but good-natured, and the menu is simple. You can even get by just with the *risotto e ossobuco*, a half-portion of each staple dish on one plate for a low price (see p81).

4 Joia, Milan

Swiss chef-owner Pietro Leeman spent time in the Orient before opening Milan's temple of vegetarian cuisine, and many of his dishes have a hint of the exotic that put them in a gourmet category. The wine list is joined by a selection of ciders and organic beers (see p91).

5 Al Pont de Ferr, Milan

Set at the foot of its name-sake iron bridge over a canal, this Navigli standby boasts on its menu: "Good cooking is a friend of the good life and an enemy of a hurried one". You can ponder this over a long, satisfying meal (see p97).

6 Aimo e Nadia, Milan

Aimo and Nadia Moroni are acknowledged as the top chefs in all Milan. They are fanatical about hunting down the very best ingredients, and it shows in such delectables as risotto with pumpkin flowers and truffles. It's a bit of a haul from the centre of the city, but it is very much worth it (see p97).

7 Villa Fiordaliso, Lake Garda

The setting is marvellous: beyond the historic Liberty-style villa (now a hotel) where D'Annunzio lived and Mussolini's mistress spent her final days, the tables are scattered about a shaded terrace lapped by lake waters. The cuisine is inventive and international, if sometimes overly minimalist *(see p122)*.

8 Il Sole di Ranco, Lake Maggiore

For more than 150 years, the Brovelli family has run an inn and *osteria* in the tiny lakeside village of Ranco. The restaurant – serving high-class creative cuisine – has summertime seating on shaded terraces. The wine list stupefies with more than 1,200 choices, and they'll set up a wine tasting to accompany your *degustazione* (tasting) menu *(see p102)*.

9 Barchetta, Lake Como

Restaurants in such touristy towns as Bellagio rarely rise to the level of quality that this has achieved under chef-owner Armando Valli and his assistant Davide Angelini. The signature

Barchetta exterior

dish is the *sinfonia degli otto sapori del lago*, a "symphony" of eight lake fishes. For dessert, try the traditional *paradel* – honey ice cream with raisins *(see p112)*.

10 I Due Roccoli, Lake Iseo

Here, when the weather is fine, you can dine on the terracotta terrace high in the hills above Iseo, with a view across a rose-fringed lawn to forested mountains beyond. The cooking is superb, and makes wonderful use of lake fish and other fresh local ingredients *(see p129)*.

I Due Roccoli

Following pages **Lake Maggiore's Isola Superiore**

AROUND
MILAN AND
THE LAKES

Milan's Historic Centre
72–81

Northern Milan
84–91

Southern Milan
92–97

Lake Maggiore
98–103

Lake Como
106–113

Lake Garda
116–123

Smaller Lakes and
Towns
124–129

MILAN AND THE LAKES

Left **Dior shop window** Centre **Cova pastry shop** Right **Galleria Vittorio Emanuele II**

Milan's Historic Centre

THE CENTRO STORICO OF MILAN *is home to the cathedral, opera house, the royal palace, art-filled private mansions and busy pedestrian*

boulevards. This historic district was once the Roman city of Mediolanum, though its boundary walls vanished long ago. As well as historic sights, the area contains a grid of shopping streets around Via Montenapoleone known as the Quadrilatero d'Oro, or "Golden Rectangle". This little area is home to some outrageously expensive boutiques, as well as haute-couture superstores and the head offices of all the biggest names in international fashion.

Via Manzoni tombstone

Sights

1. Duomo
2. Palazzo Reale
3. Santa Maria presso San Satiro
4. Pinacoteca Ambrosiana
5. Palazzo della Ragione
6. Galleria Vittorio Emanuele II
7. San Fedele
8. La Scala
9. Museo Poldi-Pezzoli
10. Museo Bagatti Valsecchi

1 Duomo

The great travel writer H V Morton *(see also p51)* likened Milan's cathedral to a forest within the city, its thickets of columns and high vaulted ceilings providing the citizens with a spot of shade *(see pp10–11)*. ❧ *Map M4*

The Duomo – Milan's "forest"

2 Palazzo Reale

Milan's Neo-Classical Royal Palace was built under the aegis of Empress Maria Theresa in the 18th century and extended in 1939–56 with the Arengario, a pair of towering pavilions on Piazza Duomo. The vast ballroom of the Arengario is open for exhibitions. In other wings are the Museo del Duomo *(see p11)* and a contemporary art museum *(see p41)*, with works by Boccioni, Modigliani, Morandi, De Chirico and De Pisis. ❧ *Map M4 • Piazza del Duomo 12*

3 Santa Maria presso San Satiro

Brilliant Renaissance architect Bramante knew the only way to squeeze a Greek cross look into a space that only allowed room for a Latin cross was to concoct a layering of stuccoes, shallow angled niches and frescoes behind the altar to give the optical illusion of a barrel-vaulted presbytery. Another notable feature of this church is a 1483 *Pietà* group by Lombard sculptor Agostino De' Fondutis *(see also pp38–9)*. ❧ *Map L4 • 7:30am–11:30am, 3:30pm–6:30pm Mon–Fri, 9am–noon, 3:30pm–7pm Sat & Sun • Free*

4 Pinacoteca Ambrosiana

Art-loving Cardinal Frederico Borromeo gave the city one of its greatest treasures when he bequeathed his private collection of works by Leonardo, Titian, Caravaggio and others, including the original cartoon for Raphael's famed *School of Athens (see pp18–19)*. ❧ *Map L4*

5 Palazzo della Ragione

Milan's 13th-century *broletto* (town hall) is a striking remnant of the Middle Ages *(see p36)*. ❧ *Map L4 • Piazza Mercanti • Open for exhibitions • Adm*

Christ Among the Doctors, Museo del Duomo, Palazzo Reale

Left **San Fedele** Right **La Scala**

6 Galleria Vittorio Emanuele II

Before modern shopping centres and malls, there were *gallerie*. These late 19th-century high-class shopping arcades were roofed by the newest architectural techno-logy of the age: steel-reinforced glass. Milan's Industrial Age-cum-Neo-Classical example connected Piazza del Duomo with La Scala and was so successful it spawned an Italy-wide trend, with copycat *gallerie* popping up in Naples, Genoa and Rome. *(See also pp36 & 56; 77–80 for shops.)* ◈ Map M3

7 San Fedele

The single nave construction of this 1559 Jesuit temple would become a blueprint for Lombard churches built in the Counter-Reformation. The Mannerist inte-rior preserves some fine paintings, including Il Cerano's *Vision of St Ignatius*, Bernardino Campi's *Four Saints and Transfiguration*, and San Peterzano's *Pietà*. The sacristy is lined by 17th-century

Galleria Vittorio Emanuele II

> **Milanese Luck**
> The central floor mosaic in the Galleria Vittorio Emanuele II sports the white-cross-on-red of the House of Savoy (representing Italy's newly crowned king who lent the gallery his name in 1868) and also a bull symbolizing Milan. According to local tradition, the Milanese ensure their good luck by stomping over the bull's testicles each time they pass.

cabinets by the Jesuit Daniele Ferrari, who also carved the pulpit. ◈ Map M3 • Piazza S Fedele/ Via T Marino • 7am–2:30pm, 4–7pm daily • Free

8 La Scala

The world's greatest opera house was built in 1776–8 under the Austrians. It boasts a sumptuous interior, excellent acoustics and a staggering list of premieres *(see p51)*. Half destroyed in World War II, La Scala again became the toast of the town in 1946 when conductor Arturo Toscanini presided over its gala reopening. Check website for up-to-date programme listings and booking information. ◈ Map M3 • Piazza della Scala • www.teatroallascala.org

9 Museo Poldi-Pezzoli

One of the greatest private collections in Italy was bequeathed to the city by Gian Giacomo Poldi-Pezzoli in 1879. Its masterpieces all date from the last half of the 15th century, including works by Piero della Francesca, Bellini, Botticelli, Pollaiolo and Mantegna. There are some 18th-century Venetian cityscapes by Canaletto and Guardi, and the *Tapestry of the Hunt* from Tabriz is celebrated. A vast collection of arms and armour is displayed in a room designed by Pomodoro in 2000 *(see also p40)*. ◈ Map M3 • *Via Manzoni 12 • 10am–6pm Tue–Sun • Adm €6*

10 Museo Bagatti Valsecchi
Two Milanese brothers created this Neo-Renaissance *palazzo* in 1883–94. They acquired as much as they could in the way of tapestries, furnishings and paintings from across Italy, and what they couldn't obtain in the original they hired an army of Lombard craftsmen to imitate. One room is copied from the ducal palace in Mantova, one from the Urbino's ducal seat, while another is lifted whole from a *palazzo* in Sondrio. The overall effect is a glorious mixture of Renaissance craftsmanship and Romantic sensibilities. ◈ Map N3 • *Via S Spirito 10/Via Gesù 5 • 1pm–5:45pm Tue–Sun • Adm €6*

Museo Poldi-Pezzoli

A Day in Central Milan

Morning

Start at 10am amid the stupendous collections of **Pinacoteca Ambrosiana**.

Work your way south to Via Torino and the jewelbox of a church, **Santa Maria presso San Satiro** *(p73)*, then walk north up Via Torino until you reach the Piazza del Duomo, Milan's vast public living room.

Continue along the piazza's western edge and divert up Via Mercanti to see the raised porticoes of **Palazzo della Ragione**. Now cross the huge **Duomo** square to enjoy the marvels of Italy's second-largest cathedral *(pp10–11)*. Don't miss exploring its roof.

Take a platter of cheese and meats in **Zucca** *(p80)* at the entrance to **Galleria Vittorio Emanuele II**, the grandest shopping arcade in Italy.

Afternoon

Exit the arcade at Piazza della Scala, flanked by the famed opera house and **Palazzo Marino** *(p76)*. Behind the latter is the church of **San Fedele**. After seeing this walk northeast past the surreal **Casa degli Omenoni** *(p76)*.

Turn left to visit the excellent **Museo Poldi-Pezzoli**, then continue north on Via Manzoni, admiring its *palazzi* and Armani boutique, until you come to Milan's prime shopping street, **Via Montenapoleone** *(p57)*.

Shoppers will spend the rest of the day here; museum hounds can take in the **Museo Bagatti Valsecchi**. Both should stop for drinks at **Cova** *(p80)*.

Around Town – Milan's Historic Centre

Left **Piazza della Scala, near Palazzo Marino** Centre **Casa degli Omenoni** Right **Casa del Manzoni**

TOP 10 Best of the Rest

1 Ca' Grande
This massive complex – originally a hospital, now part of the University of Milan – took 400 years to complete *(see also p36)*. ✪ *Map M4–5 • Via Festa del Perdono 5 • 7:30am–7:30pm Mon–Fri, 8am–11:30am Sat • Free*

2 San Nazaro Maggiore
St Ambrose's fourth basilica was overhauled in the 16th century, when Bramantino added the Cappella Trivulzio. Lanino's *Martyrdom of St Catherine of Alexandria* is among other highlights. ✪ *Map M5 • Piazza S Nazzaro • 7:30am–noon, 3:30–6:30pm Mon–Sat, 7:30am–1:15pm, 3:30–7:15pm Sun • Free*

3 Torre Velasca
This striking skyscraper is an oversized 1950s version of medieval tower design *(see p36)*. ✪ *Map M5 • Piazza Velasca 5 • No public access*

4 San Gottardo in Corte
Founded in 1336 as a chapel for the town hall. ✪ *Map M4 • Via Pecorari 2 • 8am–noon, 2–6pm Mon–Fri, 2–4pm Sat, 8am–noon Sun • Free*

5 San Sepolcro
Built in 1030 on the site of the ancient Roman forum, this church preserves a long Romanesque crypt. ✪ *Map L4 • Piazza S Sepolcro • Noon–2pm Mon–Fri • Free*

6 Palazzo Marino
Milan's Mannerist town hall *(see p37)*. ✪ *Map M3 • Piazza della Scala/Piazza S Fedele • No public access*

7 Casa degli Omenoni
Sculptor Leone Leoni's 16th-century home has a magnificent façade flanked by a Liberty-style tower *(see also p37)*. ✪ *Map M3 • Via Omenoni 3 • No public access*

8 Casa del Manzoni
Manzoni, Italy's greatest 19th-century writer *(see p50)*, lived in this Neo-Classical *palazzo*, now a museum of "Manzoniana". ✪ *Map M3 • Via Morone 1 • 02-8646-0403 • 9am–noon, 2–4pm Tue–Fri • Free*

9 The Palazzi of Via Manzoni
The boulevard from La Scala to Porta Nuova preserves many mansions from its 18th and 19th-century heyday: Brentani (No. 6), Anguissola (12), Poldi-Pezzoli *(see pp74–5)*, Gallarati Scotti (30) and Borromeo d'Adda (39–41). ✪ *Map M3–N2 • Via Manzoni • No public access*

10 Museo di Milano
Bolognini's mansion houses exhibitions on the history of Milan and its families, as well as nautical memorabilia. ✪ *Map N3 • Via Sant' Andrea 6 • 2–5:30pm Tue–Sun • Free*

Left **Prada** Centre **Gianni Versace** Right **Gianfranco Ferré**

Milanese Fashion Boutiques

1 Prada
Central outlets of the firm that transformed a handbag business into the high-fashion success story of the 1990s. ◉ *Map M3 • Galleria Vittorio Emanuele II & Via Montenapoleone 8*

2 Gianni Versace
Five floors mostly of menswear, with something for the ladies upstairs. Versace always manages to make surprises out of the ordinary. ◉ *Map N3 • Via Montenapoleone 11 (lower-price Versus label at Via San Pietro all'Orto)*

3 Trussardi
The 90-year-old Bergamo glove-making firm is now one of the top designers of supple leather goods and ready-to-wear fashions. ◉ *Map N3 • Via Sant'Andrea 5 & Piazza della Scala 5*

4 Moschino
Everything from jeans to *prêt-à-porter* from the fashion iconoclast who died young in 1994. ◉ *Map N3 • Via Sant'Andrea 12 (also Via Durini 14)*

5 Gianfranco Ferré
The former architect builds each item of clothing around a woman to accentuate her natural beauty. There's also a branch just for men. ◉ *Map N3 • Via Sant'Andrea 15 (women's); Corso Venezia 6 (men's)*

6 Missoni
Colourful knitwears from Ottavio and Rosita Missoni, who turned the fashion maxims of minimalism and basic black upside down. ◉ *Map N3 • Via Montenapoleone 8 (entrance Via Sant'Andrea)*

7 Ermenegildo Zegna
The main shop of the fashion empire that keeps a close eye on everything from the wool on the sheep to the stitching of their elegant business attire and casual wear. ◉ *Map N3 • Via P Verri 3*

8 Krizia
This Bergamo native delights in contrary fashions: colourful when black is in, miniskirts when conservative hem lines are the rage. ◉ *Map N2 • Via della Spiga 23*

9 Giorgio Armani
The first mega-department store devoted to just one fashion house – that of Milan's very own guru. ◉ *Map M2 • Via Manzoni 31*

10 Mila Schön
If you like the Italian football team's kit and the Alitalia outfits, come here for other Mila Schön designs. ◉ *Map M2 • Via Manzoni 45*

For more on Milan's top fashion designers **see p59**

77

Left **Ferragamo** Right **Dolce & Gabbana**

Other Italian Designer Shops

1 Max Mara
After more than 50 years at the top of their class in women's wear, the Maramotti family's *prêt-à-porter* fashions are more vibrant than ever. ◈ *Map N3 • Corso Vittorio Emanuele II*

2 Alessi
Tea kettles, silverware settings and other gorgeous items crafted by the top names in international industrial design, all manufactured in Lombardy. ◈ *Map N3 • Corso Matteotti 9*

3 Ferragamo
Florentine cobbler Salvatore Ferragamo raised footwear to a modern art form when he shod Hollywood stars from Greta Garbo to Sophia Loren. There's now a full clothing line. ◈ *Map N3 • Via Montenapoleone 3 (women's) and 20 (men's)*

4 Mario Buccellati
Since 1919, no two Buccelatti jewels have been the same: each gemstone and silver filigree is hand-crafted by skilled artisans. ◈ *Map N3 • Via Montenapoleone 4*

5 Etro
Etro's trademark paisley and Pegasus icons abound on silk, cashmere and the finest wools. ◈ *Map N3 • Via Montenapoleone 5 (discount branch at Via Spartaco 3)*

6 Valentino
New York's Metropolitan Museum once mounted a show of Valentino's artistic clothing.

Classy, chic and very desirable! ◈ *Map N3 • Via Montenapoleone 20*

7 Frette
Among the highest quality linens in all of Italy: drapes, pyjamas, sheets and pillows. ◈ *Map N3 • Via Montenapoeone 21*

8 Gucci
The mating "G"s that once decorated the leather goods of this firm, founded by a Florentine saddlemaker, are a thing of the past, but the quality's still topnotch. ◈ *Map N3 • Via Montenapoleone 27*

9 Laura Biagiotti
The "Queen of Cashmere" since 1972 ensures her creations are as comfy as they are elegant. The Più line is for fuller-figured women. ◈ *Map M2 • Via Borgospesso 19*

10 Dolce e Gabbana
Elegance, quality and just a little fun; D&G carry their entire line, from ready-to-wear to accessories, at these two branches. ◈ *Map N2 • Via della Spiga 2 (women's) and 26 (men's)*

Left and Centre **La Città del Sole** Right **Art magazine published by Franco Maria Ricci**

Other High-Class Shops

1 Franco Maria Ricci
Small but very prestigious Milan publisher crafting the classiest (and most expensive) coffee-table art books on the market. ◈ *Map N4 • Via Durini 19*

2 Cravatterie Nazionali
A vast selection of ties by Italy's top designers. ◈ *Map N3 • Via San Pietro all'Orto 17*

3 Mortarotti
Tired of boutique-hopping? Here's just one shop stocking a dozen major women's labels: Ferré, Missoni, Roberto Cavalli, Allegri, Eva Branca and more. ◈ *Map N3 • Via Montenapoleone 24*

4 Dmagazine
In the heart of high fashion sits a cut-price stock shop, with Fendi scarves, Armani slacks, Prada sweaters, Helmut Lang suits among the items. Check in daily for steals on the constantly rotating racks. ◈ *Map N3 • Via Montenapoleone 26*

5 Silbernagl
An eclectic mix of furnishings, porcelains, 19th- and 20th-century paintings, antique jewellery, Oriental vases and other items for decorating the well-heeled home. ◈ *Map M2 • Via Borgospesso 4*

6 Ricordi
Milan's huge subterranean branch of Italy's premiere chain of music and CD megastores –

Ricordi has come a long way since it published the music of Rossini, Verdi, Bellini and Puccini. ◈ *Map M3 • Galleria Vittorio Emanuele II*

7 Libreria Internazionale Accademia
The best place to pick up marked-down coffee-table art tomes and other bookish souvenirs. Also explore upstairs for cheap used novels in foreign languages. ◈ *Map M3 • Galleria Vittorio Emanuele II*

8 Città del Sole
Branch of a chain of toy shops that offer the best in home-made playthings. ◈ *Map L4 • Via Orefici 13*

9 Gastronomia Peck
Superlative Milanese grocers since 1883, with three vast floors of meats, cheeses, vegetables, breads, wines and other delicacies. Its pricey restaurant is nearby (see p81). ◈ *Map L4 • Via Spadari 9*

10 La Murrina
Central Milan's best shop for unique hand-made glass pieces. ◈ *Map L3 • Via Dante 14*

For more on Milan's shopping meccas and things to buy **see pp56–9**

79

Left **I Panini della Befi** Centre **Cova** Right **Caffe Martini**

TOP 10 Venues, Clubs and Cafés

1 Zucca in Galleria (Caffè Miani)
A gorgeous Liberty-style café, with views of the Duomo. Zucca holds the dubious honour of having introduced Milan to the apéritif Campari *(see also p64)*. ✎ *Map M3 • Galleria Vittorio Emanuele II/Piazza Duomo 21 • www.caffemiani.it • €*

2 Caffè Martini
This café may be overpriced but is great for Duomo views and watching the people, processions and protest rallies at Milan's heart. ✎ *Map L3 • Via dei Mercanti 21 • €*

3 La Banque
This businessmen's lunch spot (see entry 7 opposite) transforms into a yuppie disco – one of the few in Central Milan – with live music after 11pm; dress well. ✎ *Map L3 • Via Porrone 6 • 02-8699-6565 • www.labanqueweb.com*

4 La Scala
After an extensive restoration programme this magnificent opera house has recently reopened *(see p74)*. ✎ *Map M3 • Piazza della Scala • www.teatrodellascala.org*

5 Nepentha
Perennial Milan discotheque just a few blocks south of the Duomo where the chic set come to dine then dance the night away. ✎ *Map M4 • Piazza Diaz 1*

6 I Panini della Befi
Very popular *panino* bar at lunch, with umbrella-shaded tables on a pedestrian street. Stellar sandwiches, decent coffee. ✎ *Map N4 • Via Beccaria 4 • €*

7 Sant'Ambroseus
This historic café and tea room is also known for making some of the best chocolates in Italy *(see also p64)*. ✎ *Map N3 • Corso Matteotti 7 • €*

8 Cova
Nestling in the heart of Milan's boutique district since 1817, Cova offers excellent coffee and pastries *(see also p64)*. ✎ *Map N3 • Via Montenapoleone 8 • €*

9 Ice Nice
Snacks and sushi, coffee and cocktails in a nook off the main shopping area. ✎ *Map M2 • Via Borgospesso • €*

10 Conservatorio Giuseppe Verdi
Top conservatory with free concerts by Milan's philharmonic orchestra. ✎ *Map P3 • Via del Conservatorio 12; www.conservatorio-milano.com • Free*

For more entertainment venues in Milan see pp60–61

Price Categories

For a three-course meal for one with half a bottle of wine (or equivalent meal), taxes and extra charges.

€	under €20
€€	€20–€30
€€€	€30–€40
€€€€	€40–€50
€€€€€	over €50

Left **Luini** Right **Cracco-Peck sign**

TOP 10 Places to Eat

1 Trattoria da Pino
Part of a dying breed, an *osteria* of butcher-paper place-mats and simple traditional dishes tucked into a room behind the street-front bar. ⊗ *Map N4 • Via Cerva 14 • 02-7600-0532 • Closed Sun • No credit cards • €€*

2 Il Teatro del Four Seasons
The better of the Four Seasons' two restaurants is in the hotel's basement. The creative fare is exquisite and pricey *(see also p68).* ⊗ *Map N3 • Via Gesù 8 • 02-77-088 • www.fourseasons.com/milan/index.html • Closed lunch • €€€€€*

3 Don Lisander
Creative regional, Tuscan and French cuisines in palatial surroundings. ⊗ *Map M2 • Via Manzoni 12a • 02-7602-0130 • Closed Sun • €€€€€*

4 Boeucc
Hard-core Milanese cooking in an 18th-century *palazzo*, favoured by bankers and fashion bigwigs. ⊗ *Map M3 • Piazza Belgioioso 2 • 02-7602-0224 • Closed Sat and Sun lunch • €€€€€*

5 Il Cantinone
Lombard-Tuscan hybrid in two classically elegant rooms. ⊗ *Map M3 • Via Agnello 19 • 02-864-1338 • Closed Sat lunch and Sun • €€€*

6 Luini
Luini may serve only *panzerotti* (pockets of stuffed dough), but there are always long lines of people eager to eat them. ⊗ *Map M3 • Via S Radegonda 16 • 02-8646-1917 • Closed Mon • No credit cards • €*

7 La Banque
Restaurant, lounge bar and disco housed in an ex-bank. The Neo-Classical rotunda is interspersed with tables, disco balls and big screens tuned to fashion shows. ⊗ *Map L3 • Via Porrone 6 • 02-8699-6565 • €€€€€*

8 Cracco-Peck
Minimalist chic eatery complete with liveried doorman and astronomic prices *(see also p68).* ⊗ *Map L4 • Via Victor Hugo 4 • 02-876-774 • Closed Sun • €€€€€*

9 La Milanese
A 70-year-old family place offering the truest preparations of local classics in the city *(see also p68).* ⊗ *Map L4 • Via Santa Marta 11 • 02-8645-1991 • Closed Tue • €€€€*

10 Hostaria Borromei
Milanese and Italian dishes utilizing fresh seasonal ingredients. ⊗ *Map L4 • Via Borromei 4 • 02-8645-3760 • Closed Sat lunch, Sun • €€€€*

Note: *Unless otherwise stated, all restaurants accept credit cards and serve vegetarian meals*

Left **Museo di Storia Naturale** Centre **Museo dell'Ottocento** Right **Brek Restaurant**

Northern Milan

LEONARDO DA VINCI'S WORLD-FAMOUS *fading fresco*, the city's best parks and several great museums form the highlights of this area. Three museums allow you to trace art from the medieval period (at the Castello Sforzesco) through the golden era of the Renaissance (at the Brera) to the challenges of Modernism (at the Villa Reale). A further two museums give an overview of Lombard history: ancient at the Museo Archeologico and that of the 19th century in the Risorgimento. Aside from the cultural hightlights, this part of town is also a great place for bargain shoppers, from the shopwarehouses lining the street south of the central railway station to the middle-class shopping boulevard of Corso Buenos Aires.

TOP 10 Sights

1. Santa Maria delle Grazie
2. Civico Museo Archeologico
3. Castello Sforzesco
4. Parco Sempione
5. San Sempliciano
6. San Marco
7. Pinacoteca di Brera
8. Villa Belgiojoso Bonaparte/Museo dell'Ottocento
9. Cimitero Monumentale
10. Certosa di Garegnano

Fountain, Castello Sforzesco

Previous pages **Galleria Vittorio Emanuele II**

Santa Maria delle Grazie

1 Santa Maria delle Grazie

Leonardo's extraordinary fresco of the *Last Supper* adorns a wall of the convent refectory *(see pp8–9)* and is of course the chief attraction of this church. Other features include a magnificent Renaissance tribune, possibly designed by Bramante, who did the cloister and probably the main portal, too. ⊛ *Piazza S Maria delle Grazie • Map J3 • Church 7am–noon, 3–7pm Mon–Sat, 7:20am–12:15pm, 3:30–9pm Sun • Free • For Last Supper viewings see p8*

2 Civico Museo Archeologico

A few pieces in an otherwise modest collection make this a worthwhile stop. The best is the Trivulzio Cup *(see p41)*. A boulder from the Val Camonica *(see p47)*, which is adorned with 4,800-year-old Bronze Age carvings, lies in the entrance court. There's also a stunning silver platter from the mid-4th century that displays in relief the deities of earth, sky, water and the zodiac – a resounding statement of faith in the old gods at a time of encroaching Christianity. In the 15th-century cloisters, half-demolished by bombs during World War II, are a pair of brick towers from the bastions of the Imperial-era city. ⊛ *Corso Magenta 15 • Map K3 • 9am–5:30pm Tue–Sun • Adm*

3 Castello Sforzesco

Milan's vast, glowering castle complex squats at the northwest corner of the historic centre, an odd combination of oversized courtyards, lithe towers and lovely medieval nooks and crannies *(see pp16–17)*. ⊛ *Map K2*

4 Parco Sempione

Milan's only real park started life as the 15th-century ducal gardens, though its layout, laced with pathways, dates from the late 19th century. A fine little free aquarium is housed in a 1906 Liberty-style structure. There are also fountains (one by Giorgio de Chirico), exhibition halls, a sports arena and the triumphal Arco della Pace *(see p88)*. ⊛ *Piazza Sempione • Map K2 • Park 6:30am–1 hour past sunset daily • Aquarium 9:30am–5:30pm Tue–Sun • www.acquariocivico.it*

Castello Sforzesco

The Anaunia Martyrs

Three Byzantine missionaries, Sisino, Alessandro and Martirio (the name did not bode well), were sent by St Ambrose to Bishop Vigilio of Trent. Viglio assigned them to convert pagans of the Trentino Alpine valleys. But the locals of the Anaunia region were having none of it, and stoned the missionaries to death in 397, turning them into the region's first church martyrs.

5 San Sempliciano

One of four great basilicas built by St Ambrose in the 4th century (and finished by its namesake in 401) is popularly dedicated to the Anaunia Martyrs *(see box)*. The external walls are mostly original; the interior was renovated in the 11th and 12th centuries, and frescoed with a rainbow of angels and a *Coronation of the Virgin* by Bergognone in 1515. There are also patches of a late 14th-century fresco in a chapel off the choir. ◈ *Piazza S Sempliciano 7 • Map L2 • Winter: 7:15am–noon, 3–7pm daily; summer: 8am–noon, 4–7pm daily • Free*

San Marco

6 San Marco

Of the original church, finished in 1254 and dedicated to Venice's patron St Mark as a tip of the hat for Venice's help in defeating Barbarossa, all that remains is the main stone doorway, three saints in façade niches and the top of the right bell tower. The rest was overhauled in the 19th century, with care to retain some 16th-century frescoes. In the right transept, there are earlier frescoes, dating to the 13th century, which were rediscovered only in the 1950s. ◈ *Piazza S Marco 2 • Map M2 • 7am–noon, 4–7pm daily • Free*

7 Pinacoteca di Brera

In Northern Italy, Milan's painting gallery is second only to Venice's Accademia (though for sheer variety the Brera wins). Since Napoleon inaugurated the collection, it has been housed in the Jesuit's Palazzo di Brera. It's one of the regions' main Top 10, and for more on the collection – which includes works by Piero della Francesca, Raphael, Bellini, Mantegna and Caravaggio – *see pp12–15*. ◈ *Map M2*

8 Villa Belgiojoso Bonaparte/Museo dell'Ottocento

Milan's Neo-Classical (1790) "Royal Villa" housed Napoleon in 1802 and Marshal Radetzky until 1858. It is now an art gallery, with works by Romantic master Hayez, Neo-Classical sculptor Canova, Futurist Boccioni and Tuscan Macchiaioli (pseudo-Impressionist) like Lega and Fattori. Morandi, Corot, Gauguin and Van Gogh also get a look in. Marino Marini

Pinacoteca di Brera

(20th-century sculptor of happy men riding horses) gets his own wing. ◈ *Via Palestro 16* • *Map N2* • *9am–5:30pm Tue–Sun* • *Free*

9 Cimitero Monumentale

Milan's vast mid-19th-century cemetery is most popular for a pantheonic monument housing (among others) the remains of Alessandro Manzoni *(see p50)*. The grounds are filled with Art Nouveau tombs of Milan's top families – a free map shows where such notables as Arturo Toscanini rest in peace. Corners have been set aside for non-Catholic graves, and there's a monument to Jews deported by the Nazis. ◈ *Piazza Cimitero Monumentale* • *8:30am–5:15pm Tue–Sun* • *Free*

10 Certosa di Garegnano

The 14th-century Certosan abbey has largely vanished under Milan's suburbs, but its church of Santa Maria Assunta survives. It is capped with a fine late Renaissance façade, and the interior was frescoed by Daniele Crespi in 1629 with stories of the Certosan order. ◈ *Via Garegnano 28* • *7am–noon & 3–6:30pm daily* • *Free*

Museo di Storia Naturale

Touring the Great Museums of Northern Milan

Morning

🕐 There are two major museums in this itinerary, so start off early at the **Castello Sforzesco** when it opens at 9:30am. Work your way up to **San Sempliciano** around 11am, then make your way southeast to the church of **San Marco**.

🍴 Continue up Via San Marco to have lunch at one of Milan's great simple trattorie, **Latteria San Marco** *(see p91)*, then head back down the street, cross Via Pontaccio, and plunge into the vast art collections of the **Pinacoteca di Brera**.

Afternoon

If you're an art fan, you'll probably spend the rest of the afternoon at the Pinacoteca, ready for a *passeggiata* and dinner when you emerge near closing time. But if it doesn't grab you, knock off after 90 minutes and you'll have time to continue east along Via Fatebenefratelli to Piazza Cavour.

If it's between Friday and Sunday, you can turn up Via Manin to pop inside the **Palazzo Dugnani** *(p88)*; otherwise, skirt the Giardini Pubblici on Via Palestro to peruse the modern art inside the **Villa Belgiojoso Bonaparte**, then the dinosaur skeletons and wonderfully outdated 19th-century dioramas inside the **Museo di Storia Naturale** *(p88)*.

🍴 Finally, to round off a full and busy day, head for your dinner reservations at **La Terrazza** *(p91)*.

Left **Pirelli Tower** Centre **Palazzo Litta** Right **Stadio Meazza**

🔟 Best of the Rest

1 Museo del Risorgimento
Find out about the heroes of Italy's 19th-century *risorgimento* (unification) movement at this museum. ◈ *Via Borgonuovo 23 • Map M2 • 9am–1pm, 2–5:30pm Tue–Sun • Adm*

2 Porta Nuova
Piecemeal city gate incorporating ancient Roman funerary reliefs and a 13th-century marble tabernacle. ◈ *Via Manzoni/Piazza Cavour • Map N2 • Free*

3 Palazzo Dugnani
A 17th-century *palazzo* containing a Tiepolo fresco and a museum of cinema *(see p37)*. ◈ *Via Manin 2b • Map N1–2 • 3–6pm Fri–Sun • Adm*

4 Museo di Storia Naturale
Dinosaurs and taxidermied creatures are among the exhibits at the natural history museum founded in 1838. ◈ *Corso Venezia 55 • Map P2 • 9am–5pm Tue–Sun • Adm*

5 Palazzo Litta
Italy's state railway headquarters and a theatre occupy the expansive Rococo *palazzo* near the *Last Supper*. ◈ *Corso Magenta 24 • Map K3 • Open for exhibitions*

6 Museo Teatrale alla Scala
From hand-written scores to costumes, anything related to La Scala *(see p74)* can be found at this museum *(see also p41)*. ◈ *Largo Ghiringhelli 1 (Piazza Scala) • Map L/M3 • www.teatroallascala.org • 9am–noon, 1:30–5pm daily • Adm*

7 Arco della Pace
Luigi Cagnola built this magnificent triumphal arch in 1807 for Napoleon to pass through when visiting Milan. It didn't get finished quite in time and was inaugurated instead by a bemused Habsburg emperor. ◈ *Piazza Sempione • Map J1 • Free*

8 Pirelli Tower
Its reign as the world's tallest concrete skyscraper lasted less than a decade, but this wedge rising on the site of Pirelli's first tyre factory remains a symbol of Lombardy's robust economy *(see p37)*. ◈ *Piazza Duca d'Aosta • Free*

9 Ippodromo
In 1999, Milan's horse track became home to a bronze horse cast by an American foundation determined to bring to fruition Leonardo da Vinci's oft-sketched equine tribute to Lodovico il Moro. ◈ *Piazzale dello Sport 16 • 9:30am–6pm*

10 San Siro (Stadio Meazza)
"The Scala of football", shared by rivals Inter and AC Milan. ◈ *Via Piccolomini 5 • Open for matches • Adm • Museum (Gate 4, Mon–Sat, adm)*

Left **Wine, Cotti** Right **Rufus**

TOP 10 Shops

1 Emporio Isola
Discount outlet for noted clothing firms. Products are high quality and can just about be classed as haute couture, while still affordable. ☉ *Via Prina 11*

2 Corso Como 10
After serving as fashion editor for the Italian *Vogue*, Carla Sozzani opened this boutique of expensive, eminently fashionable labels on everything from clothes and accessories to books and kitchenware. There's also a café *(see p65)*. ☉ *Corso Como 10*

3 Surplus
If you feel some fashions just never go out of style, visit Milan's top shop for second-hand and reproduction vintage couture from the past four decades. ☉ *Corso Garibaldi 7 • Map L1*

4 Cotti
Nearly 1,500 Italian wines, *grappas* (brandies) and other spirits are stuffed into this 50-year-old wine and gourmet foods shop. ☉ *Via Solferino 42 • Map L1 • www.ecotecacotti.it*

5 Memphis
Shop purveying the whimsical, stunning design objects produced by Milan's Memphis group, founded in 1981 by Ettore Sottsass and other young designers. ☉ *Via della Moscova 27 • Map L1*

6 Dolce e Gabbana
Boutique for D&G's youth line (for men's and women's shops, *see p78*). Hey, if it's cool enough for Madonna to wear... ☉ *Corso Venezia 7 • Map P2*

7 Boggi
Boggi has been dressing the Milanese for years, providing them with classy men's clothing and footwear at very reasonable prices. ☉ *Corso Buenos Aires 1 • Map P1*

8 Il Drug Store
Chic designer clothing for the young and the svelte who can't yet afford Armani and Prada. ☉ *Corso Buenos Aires 28 • Map P1*

9 Vestimoda Stock
Clothing store for men and women, offering discounts on made-in-Italy fashions, often by big names. ☉ *Via M Macchi 28*

10 Rufus
Discounts on designer shoes, with some top names coming in at under €90 a pair. ☉ *Via Vitruvio 35*

Left and right **Pasticceria Marchesi**

🔟 Cafés and Entertainment Venues

1 Bar Magenta
Comfortable, Parisian-style café with outdoor seating, a decent food menu, tasty cocktails and Guinness on tap *(see also p65)*. 🚫 *Via Carducci 13 at Via Magenta • Map K3 • €*

2 Pasticceria Marchesi
A delightfully Old World café and chocolatier near the *Last Supper (see also p65)*. 🚫 *Via Santa Maria alla Porta 13 • Map K3 • €*

3 Bar Jamaica
One of half a dozen bars and *gelaterie* (ice-cream parlours) lining a pedestrianized stretch just north of the Pinacoteca. It was one of Milan's first bohemian bars, given its name by a local journalist who thought it resembled the bar in Hitchcock's *Jamaica Inn*. 🚫 *Via Brera 32 • Map L2 • €*

4 El Tombon de San Marc
Though it's touting a full menu these days, most people still head to the Brera's San Marc for its bar, beers and late hours. 🚫 *Via San Marco 20 • Map M1 • €*

5 Boulevard Café
Arty disco with live acts and throngs of hip Milanese stuffed into a narrow space and spilling out onto the street *(see also p61)*. 🚫 *Corso Garibaldi 39 • Map L2*

6 Bar Radetzky
This minimalist, down-to-business café has been around forever, best-known for a quick espresso in the morning and an *aperitivo* stop in the evening. 🚫 *Largo La Foppa 5 • Map L1 • €*

7 Bar Margherita
Comfortable, modernish lounge with deep cushions, decent snacks and good cocktails. 🚫 *Via Moscova 25 • Map L1 • €*

8 Hollywood
Fashion models and designers still hold on to the Hollywood as their own club *(see also p61)*. 🚫 *Corso Como 15 • 02-659-8996*

9 Tunnel
This warehouse under the railway station is where you come to see rock bands before they become big stars *(see also p61)*. 🚫 *Via Sammartini 30*

10 Teatro degli Arcimboldi
Originally the temporary venue for La Scala's opera and ballet companies it is way out in the industrial suburb of Bicocca – but well worth the trip for performances in a state-of-the-art theatre. 🚫 *Viale dell'Innovazione • 02-7200-3744*

Price Categories

For a three-course meal for one with half a bottle of wine (or equivalent meal), taxes and extra charges.	€ under €20
	€€ €20–€30
	€€€ €30–€40
	€€€€ €40–€50
	€€€€€ over €50

Left **Joia** Right **Sukrity**

🔟 Places to Eat

1 Pizzeria Grand'Italia
Ask a discerning Milanese to take you to the best pizzeria in town, and you'll probably end up enjoying a huge, thick slice (no full pies) here. ◎ Via Palermo 5 • Map L1 • 02-877-759 • €

2 Latteria
This Brera district trattoria has become so famous you must line up early to enjoy the simple but well-prepared Milanese fare. ◎ Via San Marco 24 • Map M1 • 02-659-7653 • Mon–Fri only • No credit cards • €€

3 La Terrazza
Mediterranean seafood in the Swiss Consulate, with views over the public gardens. ◎ Via Palestro 2 • Map N2 • 02-7600-2186 • Closed Sat & Sun • €€€€€

4 Joia
It helps that the Swiss chef at Milan's premier vegetarian restaurant creates brilliant meals even a sworn carnivore will love. ◎ Via P Castaldi 18 • Map P1 • 02-204-9244 • €€€€€

5 Sukrity
For a break from Italian fare, hit Milan's oldest Indian restaurant for excellent-value tandoori and curries. ◎ Via P Castaldi 22 • Map N1 • 02-201-315 • www.sukrity.com • €

6 Tipica Osteria Pugliese
Friendly place with simple, filling fare from Apulia in southern Italy. ◎ Via Tadino 5 • Map P1 • 02-2952-2574 • Closed Sun • €€€€€

7 Brek
Italian chain of fast-yet-excellent food. You carry a tray around to various food-prep islands, where the dishes are cooked to order. ◎ Via Lepetit 20 • 02-670-5149 • Closed Sun • €€

8 Ristorante Anzani
Unpretentious trattoria near the train station, with a menu grounded in Milanese favourites. ◎ Via Andrea Doria 44 • 02-670-4187 • Closed Sun • €€

9 Da Abele
An amazing trattoria just far enough from the tourist-filled centre to retain its local bona fides, serving up excellent fishy *primi* and roast meat *secondi* to the locals and the cognoscenti. ◎ Via Temperanza 5 • 02-261-3855 • Closed lunch and Mon • €€€

10 Pizzeria Vecchia Napoli
Neapolitans make the best pizza, and the award-winning wood-oven pizzas, simple pastas and grilled meats at this busy place go to prove it. ◎ Via Chavez 4 (off Via Padova) • 02-261-9056 • Closed Sun lunch and Mon • €

Left **Bridge over Naviglio Grande** Centre **Rotonda della Besana** Right **Abbazia**

Southern Milan

THE CITY SOUTH OF THE CENTRO STORICO CORE *is dominated by the majority of Milan's most impressive churches: ancient Sant'Ambrogio and majestic San Lorenzo Maggiore; Sant'Eustorgio, with its remarkable carvings and paintings; the Renaissance piles of Santa Maria della Passione and Santa Maria presso San Celso; and the quirky 18th-century cloverleaf of La Besana. There's also the fantastic Science and Technology Museum, housed in a former convent; within its broad scope, the museum pays due homage to Leonardo da Vinci's oft-overlooked scientific genius with an excellent display of his technical drawings and models. Further to the south stretch the Navigli canals, once a bustling centre of Milanese commerce and now host to the city's liveliest nightlife and dining scene.*

🔟 Sights

1. **Museo Nazionale della Scienza e delle Tecnica – Leonardo da Vinci**
2. **Sant'Ambrogio**
3. **San Lorenzo Maggiore**
4. **Museo Diocesano**
5. **Sant'Eustorgio**
6. **I Navigli**
7. **Santa Maria presso San Celso**
8. **Rotonda di Via Besana**
9. **Santa Maria della Passione**
10. **Abbazia di Chiaravalle**

San Lorenzo

Museo Nazionale della Scienza e delle Tecnica – Leonardo da Vinci

The National Science and Technology museum knows what draws the crowds, hence its subtitle, "Leonardo da Vinci," which refers to the wooden scale models of his inventions, which fill the main hall. However, the telecommunications work of Marconi, displays on physics, cinematography, electricity and other scientific marvels don't get short shrift either *(see also p40)*. ◈ *Via San Vittore 21 • Map J4 • www.museoscienza.org • 9:30am–4:50pm Tue–Fri, 9:30am–6:20pm Sat–Sun • Adm*

Sant'Ambrogio

Second only to the Duomo among Milan's great churches (and to many, rather more beautiful), this 4th-century basilica, with a cloistered entryway, Paleochristian mosaics, medieval carvings and late Renaissance frescoes, counts among the region's main Top 10 *(see pp20–21)*. ◈ *Map K4*

San Lorenzo Maggiore

A free-standing row of 16 Corinthian columns – once part of a 2nd-century temple – sets San Lorenzo's frontal piazza off from the road. The vast interior of the church is magnificent and sombre. It was built on a circular plan, with a ring-shaped ambulatory and matroneum, or raised women's gallery, which often marked such early churches. The Chapel of S. Aquilino, to your right as you enter the building, preserves 4th-century mosaics, a 3rd-century sarcophagus and a Roman-era portal. ◈ *Corso di Porta Ticinese 39*

Sant'Ambrogio

• *Map L5 • www.sanlorenzomaggiore.com • 8:30am–12:30pm, 2:30–6:45pm daily • Free • Chapel: 9:30am–6:30pm daily; adm*

Museo Diocesano

This museum houses important works from the treasuries of churches across Milan and Lombardy. In addition to numerous small panels by the 14th- and early 15th-century post-Giotto Gothic schools of central Italy, it preserves 17th-century Flemish tapestries and some fine altarpieces. Among these are Hayez's glowing *Crucifixion with Mary Magdalene* and Tintoretto's *Christ and the Adulterer*. ◈ *Corso di Porta Ticinese 95 • Map K5 • www.museo diocesano.it • 10am–6pm Tue–Sun • Adm*

Cloisters of Sant'Ambrogio

5 Sant'Eustorgio

The chapels opening off the right side of this ancient church were added between the 11th and 13th centuries, and frescoed in the 1300s and 1400s – Bergognone provided the triptych in the first one. The immense and impressive Arc of St Peter Martyr in the magnificent Portinari Chapel *(see p39)* was carved by Balduccio.

Sant'Eustorgio

S Piazza S Eustorgio • Map K6
• 7:30am–12:30pm, 3:30–6:30pm daily.
Museum: 10am–6pm • Free

6 I Navigli

A city as grand as Milan needed a port, so the long pool of the Darsena was dug in the 12th century, with the Naviglio Grande – a 50-km/30-mile canal stretching to the Ticino River (and thence the Po to the Adriatic) – leading into it. Today, the Navigli district is Milan's most lively, bohemian neighbourhood. Its old warehouses now contain fashionable apartments and the towpaths are lined with restaurants, clubs, bars and shops. Its streets teem nightly with foodies out for a fine meal, young folks cruising the bars and street vendors spreading out sheets and rickety tables to form an impromptu bazaar. This is the only part of the city that stays open during the dog days of August.
S South and east of Piazza XXIV Maggio • Map J3

7 Santa Maria presso San Celso

The name reflecting its proximity to the abutting Romanesque church of San Celso, this Renaissance church shot up with remarkable speed between 1493 and 1506. Its most alluring aspect is the cloister-like court before the entrance, designed by Cesare Cesarino and considered one of the best examples of early 16th-century architecture in Milan. S Corso Italia 37 • Map L6
• 7am–noon & 4–6:30pm Mon–Fri, 7am–noon & 5–7:15pm Sat–Sun • Free

8 Rotonda di Via Besana

This Greek-cross church, dating from 1713, is now used for exhibitions. It is surrounded by a small green park bounded by a lovely rosette-shaped ring of a cloister. Here, in summer, films are shown al fresco.
S Via Besana/Viale Regina Margherita
• Map P5 • Open for exhibitions

9 Santa Maria della Passione

Originally a modest Greek-cross church of 1486–1530, it was elongated with a massive nave and deep chapel niches in 1573 to make it the second largest church in Milan. Its interior is dominated by the work of Daniele Crespi: a portrait of San Carlo in the first chapel on the left, most of the Passion series below

Rotonda di Via Besana

the cupola at the crossing, the organ doors and throughout the Museo della Basilica (a series of rooms that open to the right of the altar). ◈ *Via Bellini 2 • Map P3 • 7am–noon, 3:30–6pm daily • Free*

10 Abbazia di Chiaravalle
A countryside abbey now surrounded by the roar of suburban Milan, Chiaravalle has survived the centuries since its construction (between 1172 and 1221) remarkably well. Its lovely Romanesque architecture is enhanced by 15th- and 16th-century murals and a Luini *Madonna with Child* in the right transept.
◈ *Via S Arialdo 102 • 9–11:30am, 3–6:30pm Tue–Sat, 3–4:30pm Sun • Free*

Abbazia di Chiaravalle

A Day with Leonardo

Morning

🕐 To spend time with the great Renaissance genius you must transgress the division between north and south Milan.

Begin the day's itinerary at the Cordusio metro stop, then walk west on Via Meravigli three blocks to the corner with Via S Maria alla Porta for a cappuccino at **Pasticceria Marchesi**. Continue west, and pop into the **Museo Archeologico** *(p85)* for 20 minutes of historical musing.

Make reservations long in advance for a 10am admission to the *Last Supper* *(p85)*. Take time to fully appreciate Leonardo's art.

Go east along Corso Magenta to Via Carducci to relax at the Art Nouveau **Bar Magenta** *(see p90)* and enjoy an early lunch.

Afternoon/Evening

Turn down Via Carducci four long blocks to Via San Vittore (you'll see across the street the Pusterla di S Ambrogio, a remnant of the medieval city gates) and turn right for the **Museo della Scienza** *(p93)*.

At around 3:30pm double back along Via S Vittore to S Ambrogio. Trek down Via Edmondo De Amicis to Corso della Porta Ticinese, where your first stop is the magnificent **San Lorenzo Maggiore** *(p93)*. Peruse the works in the **Museo Diocesano**, then continue to **Sant'Eustorgio**.

A block south brings you into the bar and restaurant zone of the **Navigli**, ready for a post-itinerary drink and a superb meal *(pp96–7)*.

Left **Discount shopfront** Right **Porta Ticinese shoppers**

🔟 Shops and Nightspots

1 Specchio di Alice
A thrift shop with slightly used and reconditioned clothing for men and women. Great leather jackets and retro items.
◈ *Corso di Porta Ticinese 64 • Map K5*

2 Floretta Coen Misul
Bargain-basement prices on brand-name clothing (Missoni, Ferrè, Yves St Laurent). Major label dresses under €150, suits under €200. ◈ *Via San Calocero 3 • Map J5*

3 Biffi
All the major labels for men and women, including whatever's hot this season. No great deals, but a remarkably broad selection.
◈ *Corso Genova 6 • Map J5*

4 El Brellin
A restaurant, Naviglio-front tavern, part-time live music venue and proud owner of a miniscule canal that was, in times gone by, used by Milanese washerwomen.
◈ *Vicolo dei Lavandai/Alzaia Naviglio Grande 14 • Map J6 • 02-5810-1351 • Closed Sun • €€€€€*

5 Birreria La Fontanella
Large, noisy room where the youth down beers from glasses so tall and unwieldy they require wooden stands to support them.
◈ *Alzaia Naviglio Pavese 6 • Map K6 • 02-837-2391 • Closed Mon • €*

6 Scimmie
A veteran of Navigli nightlife – a jazz bar with quality live acts nightly, a restaurant and pizzeria, and a barge for al fresco fun.
◈ *Via Asciano Sforza 49 • Map K6 • 02-8940-2874 • www.scimmie.it • €*

7 Grand Café Fashion
Models, upmarket yuppies, flashy trendoids and people who'd like to be/meet all of the above cram the Grand's garden and disco. ◈ *Corso di Porta Ticinese 60 • Map K5 • 02-8940-2997 • Closed Mon • €€*

8 Limelight
A post-modern disco owned by a group of Premier League footballers. The DJs spin everything from revival pop to salsa.
◈ *Via Castelbarco 11 • 02-5831-0682 • €*

9 Il Salvagente
The best discount outlet in Milan, with two floors of Italian, French and American fashion at about 50% discount. Additional sales in January and June.
◈ *Via Fratelli Bronzetti 16*

10 Rolling Stone
The undisputed king of live rock music has weathered the past 20 years with its reputation firmly intact. ◈ *Corso XXII Marzo 32 • 02-733-172 • www.rollingstone.it • Closed Sun and Mon • €€*

Price Categories

For a three-course	€ under €20
meal for one with half	€€ €20–€30
a bottle of wine (or	€€€ €30–€40
equivalent meal), taxes	€€€€ €40–€50
and extra charges.	€€€€€ over €50

Left **Premiata Pizzeria** Right **Trattoria Aurora**

Places to Eat

1 Ponte Rosso
Ignoring the hipness of Naviglio, Ponte Rosso serves up hearty dishes from Milan and Trieste. ۞ Ripa di Porta Ticinese 23 • Map J6 • 02-837-3132 • Closed Sun & Mon lunch • €€€€

2 Al Pont de Ferr
Of Naviglio's many great eateries, this is one of the few whose renown is entirely due to the quality of food (see also p68). ۞ Ripa di Porta Ticinese 55 • Map J6 • 02-8940-6277 • €€€€

3 Le Vigne
A mix of local and Piemontese cuisines. The caramelle di ricotta e spinaci (like ravioli) can't be beaten. ۞ Ripa di Porta Ticinese 61 • Map J6 • 02-837-5617 • Closed Sun • €€€

4 Premiata Pizzeria
Navigli's most popular pizzeria, with semi-industrial décor and a coveted terrace. Book ahead. ۞ Via Alzaia Naviglio Grande 2 • Map K6 • 02-8940-0648 • Closed Tue lunch • €

5 Asso di Fiori
Its theme is simple: include Italian cheeses in as many dishes as possible, culminating in a stupendous cheese platter. ۞ Alzaia Naviglio Grande 54 • Map K6 • 02-8940-9415 • Closed Sun • €€€

6 Trattoria Famiglia Conconi
A short and tasty seasonal menu at this family-run restaurant. Good wine list too. ۞ Alzaia Naviglio Grande 62 • Map K6 • 02-8940-6587 • Closed Mon • €€€€

7 Grand Hotel
Tucked down an alleyway off Viale Liguria, here you can enjoy inventive, exquisite Milanese-Mantovana cuisine on a garden terrace. ۞ Via Asciano Sforza 75 • Map K6 • 02-8951-1586 • Closed Mon • €€€

8 Sadler
Claudio Sadler, perhaps the top chef in Milan, melds modern techniques with regional cuisine in a contemporary setting. ۞ Via Troilo 14 • 02-5810-4451 • Closed Sun • €€€€€

9 Trattoria Aurora
The fixed-price menu at this temple of Piemontese cuisine is incredible value and reason enough to come. Yet the vine-shaded setting is the restaurant's coup de grace. ۞ Via Savona 23 • Map J5 • 02-8940-4978 • Closed Mon • €€€€

10 Aimo e Nadia
Pricey and out in the suburbs, yet Aimo and Nadia (a Tuscan-born husband-and-wife team) run this place with exquisite taste throughout, and it ranks among Milan's very, very best (see also p68). ۞ Via P Montecuccoli 6 • 02-416-886 • Closed Sat lunch and Sun • €€€€€

Left **Isla Madre, Isole Borromee** Centre **Santa Caterina del Sasso** Right **Rocca di Angera**

Lake Maggiore

THE WESTERNMOST OF ITALY'S GREAT LAKES *straddles the Lombardy-Piemonte border and pokes its head into Switzerland. The southern half was from the 15th century a fiefdom of the powerful Borromeo clan. Maggiore's development as a holiday retreat for Europeans began in 1800 when Napoleon's Simplon highway from Geneva to Milan skirted its shores. Maggiore is neither as resorty as Garda nor as breathtaking as Como, and while the triplet Borromean Islands are stunning, few of Maggiore's other diversions can compare. Still, all this can play in Maggiore's favour if you're looking to avoid the over-development of Garda and the crowds of Como.*

Statue of Carlo Borromeo, Arona

Sights

1. Arona
2. Rocca di Angera
3. Stresa
4. Santa Caterina del Sasso
5. Isole Borromee
6. Verbania
7. Cannero Riviera
8. Cannobio
9. Ascona
10. Locarno

Stresa

1 Arona

This sprawling modern town was once a stronghold of the Borromeo family, but its fortress was razed by Napoleon. The only lasting monument to the great family is a disconcertingly enormous 17th-century bronze statue of San Carlo Borromeo. Clamber up a ladder-like stair to the head of the 23-m (75-ft) colossus to peek out through his pupils at the 17th-century church below. The road leading to this shrine was meant to be lined with 15 devotional chapels, but only two were finished. ✎ *Map A3 • Tourist info: Piazzale Duca d'Aosta • 0322-243-601*

Arona

2 Rocca di Angera

This medieval castle, a Borromeo fortress since 1449, preserves a hall of crude frescoes (1342–54), which count among the oldest surviving Lombard-Gothic works on a non-religious subject. Wooden staircases lead to the tower and lake views. Most of the rooms now house a Doll Museum, with its splendid collection of Japanese figures and 18th- and 19th-century European examples *(see also p42)*. ✎ *Angera • Map A3 • 0331-931-300 • Mar–Sep: 9:30am–5:30pm daily; Oct & Nov 9:30am–5pm daily • Adm*

3 Stresa

The gateway to the Isole Borromee *(see p100)* is a pretty lakeside burg that offers hotels, a grid of trattoria-lined pedestrian streets and quite a good summer music festival *(see p52)*. Just south of town, the Villa Pallavicino has a botanical garden and small zoo. ✎ *Map A3 • Tourist info: 0323-313-08 • www. parcozoopallavicino.it*

4 Santa Caterina del Sasso

In thanks for being saved from a shipwreck in the 13th century, a local merchant built a chapel into the cliff face above the treacherous, deepest part of the lake. There are some frescoes, but the greatest attraction is the setting itself *(see also p42)*. ✎ *Outside Leggiuno • Map B3 • 8:30am–noon, 2:30–6pm daily (weekends only in winter) • Free*

Rocca di Angera

Around the Region – Lake Maggiore

Left **Gardens, Isole Borromee** Right **Cannero Riviera**

5 Isole Borromee

From the 1650s to today, the trio of tiny islands in the middle of Lake Maggiore has drawn admirers for the gracious palaces and ornate gardens built by the Borromeo family, who still own everything but the fishing village on Isola Superiore. The islands are among Lombardy's top attractions *(see pp22–3).* ◈ *Map A2/3*

6 Verbania

In 1939 Mussolini gave the ancient Roman name "Verbania" to a group of villages here that include little Suna, industrialized Intra and Pallanza, an important town in the Middle Ages. Pallanza's main sight is the landscaped garden of Villa Taranto *(see p44),* while its Palazzo Viani-Dugnani houses a collection of landscape paintings. ◈ *Map A2 • Tourist info: Corso Zanitello 6–8 • 0323-503-249*

7 Cannero Riviera

Despite its northern locale, this sheltered promontory has a truly Mediterranean clime, enabling citrus trees and camellias to flourish. The lake vistas, steep medieval streets and 18th-century houses give it a pleasant feel. Most striking

The Bloody Mazzardits

In the 15th century, the five Mazzarditi brothers built Cànnero's castle-islets as a base from which to rob villages and ships. The brothers kept any captured women chained inside, but murdered the men. In 1414, Cànnero sent 500 soldiers to attack the castle. Four brothers escaped, the fifth was drowned; his ghost is said to still haunt the ruins.

are the scraps of islands just offshore, sprouting glowering castles built by lake pirates in the 1400s *(see box)* and used by the Borromeo clan as a defensive line against the Swiss. ◈ *Map B2 • Tourist info: Via Angelo Orsi 1 • 0323-788-943 • Winter: 3–6pm Mon, Thu, Fri*

8 Cannobio

By the Swiss border at the base of a rushing mountain stream near the pretty Orrido di Santa

Cannobio

Anna gorge, Cannobio dates back more than 3,000 years, though its steep, crooked pebble lanes and old plastered buildings are mainly medieval. The harbour is filled with restaurant tables in summertime. ◍ *Map B2 • Tourist info: Viale Vittorio Veneto 4 • 0323-71-212 • www.cannobio.net*

9 Ascona

Locarno's neighbouring town on the Swiss end of the lake has been a favourite haunt of such cultural giants as Kandinsky, Freud and Thomas Mann. It has a split personality: there's a Harley rally and Jazz festival in July, and a Rolls Royce gathering and classical music concerts in September. The streets are lined with top-end boutiques and sights such as the 16th-century church Santi Pietro e Paolo. Up on the mountainside is Monte Verità. From the late 1800s to the 1940s this was a utopian community that housed artists, vegetarians and nudists. ◍ *Map B2 • Tourist info: Casa Serodine on the lakeside Via Albarelle • 0041-917-910-091*

10 Locarno

Sadly, most of this Swiss city at the northern end of the lake was rebuilt along modern Swiss lines of concrete, glass and steel. What remains of the medieval city, however, is worth crossing the border for. The 14th-century Castello Visconteo is a highlight, as is the Santuario della Madonna del Sasso (1497), which preserves paintings by Bramantino and Ciseri (avoid the long climb by taking the cable car). The Arps (20th-century artists Jean, Hans and Margherita) donated many works to a modern art gallery installed in the 17th-century Casa Rusca. ◍ *Map B1 • Tourist info: in the Casino on Piazza Grande • 0041-917-910-091*

A Day on Lake Maggiore

Morning

🕐 Be at the **Stresa** ferry dock *(see p99)* by 10am and buy a day pass for island hopping as well as admission tickets for the **Isole Borromee** sights.

Ride to **Isola Bella** first to spend two hours exploring the collections of the **Borromeo Palace** and the intricate gardens above it. Then catch the 12:25pm ferry for the short hop to the **Isola Superiore**, where you can settle into a lakeside table on **Verbano's** terrace for lunch with a view (book ahead of time, *see p102*).

Mid-Afternoon

Wander the tourist/fishing village after lunch before continuing on the boat to **Isola Madre**.

The **Borromeo Villa** on Madre takes only a half hour to wander, but the vast botanical gardens surrounding it are a delight, thick with exotic flora and populated by colourful exotic birds. The multilingual map handed out explains many of the rare specimens and is remarkably informative too.

Try to catch a return ferry that stops on the mainland at Lido/Funivia for **Montarrone** – one stop before Stresa proper. Get off here and stroll along the little-used waterfront promenade for the final 20-minute walk back to downtown Stresa. You will be rewarded with a lovely late-afternoon view of the islands on your left, and romantically crumbling, abandoned villas on your right.

Price Categories

For a three-course meal for one with half a bottle of wine (or equivalent meal), taxes and extra charges.

€	under €20
€€	€20–€30
€€€	€30–€40
€€€€	€40–€50
€€€€€	over €50

Left **Osteria degli Amici** Right **Verbano**

Places to Eat

1 Osteria degli Amici, Stresa

This convivial spot in the back streets has some outdoor tables and a menu ranging from pizza to freshly caught lake fish. ✆ *Via Bolognaro 31 • Map A3 • 0323-30-453 • Closed Wed, mid-Dec–Feb • €€€*

2 Ristorante del Pescatore, Stresa

Tucked away in the upper reaches of town, this restaurant is popular for fish dinners and a Valencian paella (for two or more only) for which it's best to book ahead. ✆ *Vicolo del Poncivo 3 (off Via Bolognaro) • Map A3 • 0323-31-986 • Closed Thu, Dec–Jan • €€€€€*

3 Piemontese, Stresa

Stresa's top restaurant piles on the elegance with bow-tied service and a wood-panelled dining room. What's best, though, is the vine-shaded cobbled courtyard, where you can enjoy hearty local dishes with a modern twist. ✆ *Via Mazzini 25 • Map A3 • 0323-30-235 • Closed Mon, Dec–Jan • €€€€€*

4 Verbano, Isola Superiore (Isola dei Pescatori)

The hotel's restaurant *(see entry 4, opposite)* is set on a terrace at the tip of the island, with great views. Regional dishes are very good and reasonably priced. ✆ *Map A3 • 0323-32-534 • Closed Dec–Feb • €€€€*

5 Milano, Verbania-Pallanza

Verbania's best restaurant serves classic Piemontese dishes and lake fish in lovely grounds.

✆ *Corso Zanitello 2 • Map A2 • 0323-556-816 • Closed Mon dinner, Tue • €€€€€*

6 Boccon di Vino, Verbania-Suna

Laid-back little *osteria* serving home-made pastas and hearty seconds under vaulted ceilings. ✆ *Via Troubetzkoy 86 • Map A2 • 0323-504-039 • Closed Wed & Thu lunch • €€€*

7 Lo Scalo, Cannobio

The best of Cannobio's restaurants offers Piemontese cooking with inventive touches and a generous use of vegetables and lake fish. ✆ *Piazza Vittorio Emanuele II 32 • Map B2 • 0323-71-480 • Closed Mon, Tue lunch, mid-Jan–mid-Feb • €€€€€*

8 Il Sole, Ranco

Regional specialities and ancient recipes in a modern room filled with New Age music *(see p69)*. ✆ *Piazza Venezia 5 • Map A3 • 0331-976-507 • Closed Tue & Dec–Jan • €€€€€*

9 La Vecchia Arona, Arona

Franco Carrera is an enthusiastic and innovative reinterpreter of "traditional" dishes. The menu changes daily in accordance with his whim. ✆ *Via Marconi 17 • Map A3 • 0322-242-469 • Closed Fri • €€€€*

10 Trattoria Campagna, Arona

A country trattoria in the hills above Arona, with seasonal menu composed of excellent home-made pastas and stuffed game meats. ✆ *Via Vergante 12 • Map A3 • 0322-57-294 • Closed Mon dinner & Tue • €€€€*

Note: *Unless otherwise stated, all restaurants accept credit cards and serve vegetarian dishes*

Price Categories

For a standard, double room per night (with breakfast if included), taxes and extra charges.	€ under €110
	€€ €110–€160
	€€€ €160–€210
	€€€€ €210–€270
	€€€€€ over €270

Left **Grand Hotel, Locarno** Right **Il Sole**

🔟 Places to Stay

1 Grand Hôtel des Iles Borromées, Stresa
One of Italy's top hotels (with a starring role in Hemingway's *A Farewell to Arms*), this is as sumptuous as you'd expect at the prices. ⍟ *Corso Umberto I 67 • Map A3 • 0323-938-938 • www.borromees.it • €€€€€*

2 La Palma, Stresa
Almost luxury-level living at relatively moderate prices: lake views from balconies, oversize marble bathrooms, pool. ⍟ *Corso Umberto I 33 • Map A3 • 0323-32-401 • www.hlapalma.it • Closed Dec–Feb • €€€*

3 Primavera, Stresa
A small hotel in the pedestrian centre of Stresa. Simple rooms have the basic amenities. ⍟ *Via Cavour 30 • Map A3 • 0323-31-286 • www.stresa.it • Closed winter (exc Christmas and New Year) • €*

4 Verbano, Isola Superiore (Isola dei Pescatori)
A lovely retreat. The much-requested rooms at the front overlook the restaurant *(see entry 4 on previous page)*. ⍟ *Map A3 • 0323-30-408 • www.hotelverbano.it • Closed Jan • €€€*

5 Grand Hotel Majestic, Verbania-Pallanza
One of Maggiore's top hotels since 1870, with spacious rooms, courtyard and lawn. ⍟ *Via Vittorio Veneto 32 • Map A2 • 0323-504-305 • www.grandhotelmajestic.it • Closed Nov–Mar • €€€€*

6 Pironi, Cannobio
The wedge-shaped 15th-century building has a frescoed loggia and splashing fountain. Rooms exude antique charm. ⍟ *Via Marconi 35 • Map B2 • 0323-70-624 • www.pironihotel.it • Closed Nov–Mar • €€*

7 Il Portico, Cannobio
Modern hotel in a quiet corner of town. Its porticoed restaurant and best rooms overlook the lake. ⍟ *Piazza Santuario 2 • Map B2 • 0323-70-598 • www.hotelilportico.com • €*

8 Grand Hotel, Locarno
In 1925, European leaders met in this grand dame of a hotel to sign the Locarno Treaty (which failed to prevent World War II). Public spaces are Belle Époque genteel; rooms are modern. ⍟ *Via Sempione 17 • Map B1 • 41-091-743-0282 • www.grand-hotel-locarno.ch • €€*

9 Il Sole, Ranco
The best lodgings on the east shore. Rooms mix antique furnishings with modern comforts, and there's a great restaurant *(see entry 8 on previous page)*. ⍟ *Piazza Venezia 5 • Map A3 • 0331-976-507 • www.relaischateaux.com • Closed Dec–Feb • €€€€*

10 Conca Azzurra, Ranco
A modern lakeside retreat with a pool and tennis courts. ⍟ *Via Alberto 53 • Map A3 • 0331-976-526 • www.concazzurra.it • Closed mid-Dec–mid-Feb • €€*

Note: Unless otherwise stated, all hotels accept credit cards and have air-conditioning and en-suite bathrooms

Left **Statue, Villa Melzi, Bellagio** Centre **Piazza del Duomo, Como** Right **Ferry, Tremezzo**

Lake Como

*C*OMO IS THE BEAUTY QUEEN *of the Italian lakes, the turquoise and sapphire waters of its three arms – 50 km (30 miles) long, but rarely more than 2 km (1 mile) wide – backed by the snow-capped peaks of the pre-Alps. The area's diversity stretches from the windsurfers and alpine vistas in the north to the busy towns capping the southern arms, such as Como, a Roman town with a glorious cathedral and silk industry, and Lecco, full of literary associations with Manzoni's great novel I Promessi Sposi. For centuries Lake Como has seduced visitors and drawn in the wealthy to line its shores with gracious villas and verdant gardens; it has also inspired composers (Liszt, Verdi, Bellini) and writers such as Byron, Shelley and Wordsworth.*

Basilica di Sant'Abbondio

🔟 Sights

1. **Duomo, Como**
2. **Basilica di Sant'Abbondio, Como**
3. **Brunate Funicular, Como**
4. **Villa Balbianello, Lenno**
5. **Villa Serbelloni, Bellagio**
6. **Villa Melzi, Bellagio**
7. **Villa Carlotta, Tremezzo**
8. **Villa Monastero, Varenna**
9. **Villa Cipressi, Varenna**
10. **Abbazia di Piona**

Caffè Rossi, Bellagio

Previous pages **Bellagio on Lake Como**

Duomo, Como

architecturally, to the Westwerk style of medieval Germany. The apse is gorgeously frescoed with a series of Biblical scenes. ✪ *Via Sant'Abbondio (off Viale Innocenzo XI) • Map C3 • 9am–5pm daily • Free*

1 Duomo, Como

Como's statue-clad cathedral was begun in 1396, but not capped with its Juvara-designed dome until 1740. On the façade, the pilasters are lined with saints and the main door is flanked by the seated figures of two local ancient scholars, Pliny the Elder and his nephew Pliny the Younger. The interior preserves an intricately carved and painted wooden altarpiece of 1492 and nine fabulous 16th-century tapestries, produced in Flemish, Florentine and Ferrarese workshops. ✪ *Piazza del Duomo • Map C3 • 031-265-244 • 7am–noon, 3–7pm • Free*

2 Basilica di Sant'Abbondio, Como

Standing forlorn in Como's industrial suburbs, this stony Romanesque church retains a pair of bell towers and an extended choir that links it,

3 Brunate Funicular, Como

The classic journey to this hillside village is to take a short walk from Como's harbour to the funicular station, then ride the funicular up to Brunate. You're rewarded with vistas over Como and the lake, and the starting point of many trails into the surrounding hills. ✪ *Piazza A De Gasperi • Map C3 • 031-303-608 • Half-hourly 6:30am–midnight daily (to 10:30pm in winter) • Adm*

4 Villa Balbianello, Lenno

The statue-lined balustrades fringed with flowers that outline the terraced gardens of this 1784 villa have caught the eye of many a film director. The best approach is by boat from Lenno, though on Tuesday, Saturday and Sunday it's also accessible by foot. To tour the villa itself (pricey) you must book in advance. For more, see p45. ✪ *Lenno • Map C2 • 0344-56-110 • 10am–1pm, 2–6pm Tue, Thu & Fri; 10am–6pm Sat, Sun & hols • Adm*

Villa Balbianello

For places to stay around Lake Como see p113

Left **Bellagio's promontory** Right **Villa Melzi**

Around the Region – Lake Como

Villa Serbelloni, Bellagio
Bellagio's promontory has been prime real estate for millennia. Pliny the Younger had a villa named "Tragedy" here (it matched a "Comedy" home on the far shore), replaced by a castle in the Middle Ages, then a Stagna family villa in the 15th century. The last Stagna left it to his best friend Serbelloni in 1788. Serbelloni proceded to rebuild the villa as a summer residence to the main house down in the village (now the Villa Serbelloni hotel, *see p113*). In 1959, the summer home passed to the Rockefeller Foundation, and now visiting scholars can live and study here for short periods. It is not open to the public, but you can tour the gardens *(see p44)*. ✪ *Piazza della Chiesa, Bellagio • Map C2 • 031-951-555 • Tours Apr–Oct: 11am and 4pm Tue–Sun • Adm*

Villa Carlotta

Como Silk
Como has been Italy's silk capital since 1510. While they now import the spun thread from China, the fabrics Como's artisans weave is still the most sought-after by Milan's top designers. There are shops and warehouse stores all around town hawking silk wares. In the city outskirts there is even a Museum of Silk at Via Valleggio 3 (031-303-180; www.museosetacomo.com).

Villa Melzi, Bellagio
The meticulous gardens surrounding the Neo-Classical home of Francesco Melzi d'Eril, Napoleon's man in Italy, are now open to the public *(see also p44)*. ✪ *Via P Carcano • Map C2 • 031-950-204 • Mid-Mar–Oct: 9am–6pm daily • Adm*

Villa Carlotta, Tremezzo
One of the most sumptuous villas on the lake, with exquisitely landscaped gardens. Unusually, you can tour the art-strewn villa here, as well as its wonderful surrounds *(see also p44)*. ✪ *Tremezzo • Map C2 • 0344-40-405 • www.villacarlotta.it • Apr–Sep: 9am–6pm daily; 18–31 Mar & Oct: 9–11:30am & 2–4:30pm daily • Adm*

Villa Monastero, Varenna
This blissful villa – a former convent – has gardens that stretch right down to the banks of the lake, wonderfully shaded throughout by the canopies of

Villa Monastero

cypresses and palms *(see also p45)*. ◈ *Via IV Novembre • Map C2 • www.villamonastero.it • Mar–Oct: 9am–7pm daily • Adm*

9 Villa Cipressi, Varenna
The Cipressi villa has been altered throughout its 600-year life, though what you see today is largely 19th century. Its gardens are modest compared to others (including neighbour Villa Monastero), but unlike most other villas on the lake, you can make this one your home – temporarily – since it's now a hotel *(see p113)*. For more, *see p45.* ◈ *Via IV Novembre 18 • Map C2 • 0341-830-113 • Mar–5 Nov: 9am–7pm daily (to 6pm Mar–Jun) • Adm*

10 Abbazia di Piona
At the tip of the Ogliasca peninsula sits this Benedictine abbey, cloaked in silence. The abbey was founded in the 9th century, and the little church has Romanesque carvings decorating the water stoups and the capitals and bases of the columns in the quiet cloister. The monks distil – and sell – some potent liqueurs too. ◈ *Signposted off the lake road • Map C2 • 0341-940-331 • 9am–noon & 2–6pm daily • Free*

Town Hopping

Morning

To cruise the lake you can buy point-to-point tickets, or peruse the single-ticket cruises that visit several towns and may include villa admissions. This itinerary assumes you have already checked out Como's sights before spending the night in **Bellagio**.

Begin the next day with a cappuccino at Bellagio's **Caffè Rossi** across from the dock before boarding the 10:30am boat to **Villa Carlotta**, where you have an hour to visit the collection of art and lush gardens of the lake's greatest villa.

Catch the ferry down to Isola Comacina to dig into a sumptuous feast at the **Locanda** *(see p112)*. After a second helping of their "spiked" coffee, you'll have a bit of time to work off the meal by exploring the island's overgrown church ruins before grabbing the boat back up the lake to **Varenna**.

Mid-afternoon

Continue walking off the big lunch by climbing up to the romantic, panoramic Castello di Vezio above town, then descend and pop into Varenna's little churches. Poke around the gardens of **Villa Monastero**, then finally head down to the lakefront arcade for a short stroll then a meal by the water at the splendid **Vecchia Varenna** *(see p112)*.

Unless you decide to spend a relaxing night in quiet and little visited Varenna, make sure you finish dinner before 9pm, when the last ferry leaves for Bellagio.

Left **Bellagio** Centre **Varenna** Right **Menaggio**

🔟 Lakeside Towns

1 Bellagio
A popular town, containing the gardens of villas Serbelloni and Melzi, a Romanesque church, a café-lined harbour front and a pretty warren of medieval alleys *(see p108)*. ⊗ *Map C2 • Info at ferry dock on Piazza Mazzini • 031-950-204 • www.bellagiolakecomo.com*

2 Como
Italy's silk capital was founded by the Romans and has a spectacular cathedral *(see p107)*, a handful of modest museums, lots of boutiques and two ancient churches. ⊗ *Map C3 • Tourist info: IAT, Piazza Cavour 17; 031-330-0111; www.lakecomo.org • Local info: to the right of the Duomo; 031-264-215*

3 Varenna
Arguably, Varenna makes a better base for exploring the lake than crowded Bellagio. It has ferry links with the major towns and everything from frescoed churches to lovely walks *(see pp108–9)*. ⊗ *Map C2 • Info at Piazza Venini 1 • 0341-830-367*

4 Menaggio
A pleasant little resort on the main ferry lines, with some modest Baroque churches. ⊗ *Map C2 • Tourist info: Piazza Garibaldi 8 • 0344-32-924*

5 Tremezzo
A tiny resort whose main claim to fame is the Villa Carlotta *(see p108)*. ⊗ *Map C2 • Tourist info: IAT, Via Regina 3; 0344-404-93*

6 Lecco
The capital of the lake's southeastern arm is famous for sights related to native writer Alessandro Manzoni, who set parts of his *I Promessi Sposi (see p50)* in the suburban hamlet of Olate. ⊗ *Map D3 • Info at Via N Sauro 6 • 0341-362-360 • www.aptlecco.com*

7 Gravedona
The town has two excellent medieval churches: Santa Maria del Tiglio and, up on the hillside, Santa Maria delle Grazie. ⊗ *Map C2 • Info at Piazza Cavour • 0344-89-637*

8 Bellano
On Piazza S. Giorgio sits the black-and-white striped façade of Santi Nazaro e Celso. A steep street leads to the entrance of the dramatic Orrido gorge. ⊗ *Map C2 • Info at Via V Veneto 23 • 0341-821-124*

9 Lenno
Don't miss the 11th-century Santo Stefano and neighbouring baptistry. Just north of town, in Mezzegra, a black cross marks the spot where Mussolini was shot by partisans. ⊗ *Map C2 • Info at town hall, Via S Stefano 7 • 0344-55-147*

10 Civate
On tiny Lake Annone in the Brianza triangle between Como and Lecco, Civate is the access point to San Pietro al Monte, a wonderful 11th-century monastic complex. ⊗ *Map D3 • Monastery: 0341-319-1501; summer 9am–4pm; winter 9am–noon and 2–3pm • Free*

 Browse www.fromitaly.net/lakecomo and www.lakecomo.org for more information about Como's lakeside towns

Left **Cycling** Centre **Windsurfing** Right **Divina Commedia**

Things to Do

1 Playing a Round of Golf
Definitely make a round of the 18 holes at Circolo Villa D'Este and check out the course of Golf Club Menaggio & Cadenabbia. ◈ *Circolo, Montorfano, 031-200-200* • *Menaggio & Cadenabbia 0344-32-103*

2 Mountain Biking
The forested hills of Bellagio's peninsula make perfect mountain-bike country. Saddle up at a local hire shop. ◈ *Bike hire: Cavalcalario Club, Gallasco, 031-964-814* • *Rullo Bike, Via Grandi, Como, 031-263-025, www.rullobike.com*

3 Windsurfing
The strong winds of the lake's northern end draw an international crowd of windsurfers. ◈ *Equipment hire: Windsurfcenter Domaso, 380-700-0010, www.breva.ch* • *Unione Sportiva Derviese, Dervio, 0341-804-159, www.usderviese.it*

4 Horse Riding
Choose between English- or Western-style saddles and trek through mountain valleys off the Menaggio-Porlezza Road. ◈ *Trekking centre: Cenuta La Torre, 338-894-7814*

5 Climbing
Rock climb in the mountains ringing the lake's southeastern end. ◈ *Info at CAI, Via Papa Giovanni XXIII, Lecco* • *0341-363-588, www.cailecco.it*

6 Kayaking
Get a different perspective on Como's fabled coastline,

peeking into private lakeside gardens from a kayak or canoe. ◈ *Boat hire: Cavalcalario Club, Gallasco (see entry 2)* • *Società Canottieri, Via Nullo 2, Lecco, 0341-364-273, www.canottieri.la.it*

7 Visiting the Divina Commedia, Bellagio
The coolest pub in Bellagio, with the top floor a cloud-frescoed "Paradise"; the ground floor "Purgatory"; and the tiny basement a papier-mâché "Inferno". ◈ *Salita Mella 43–45* • *031-951-680* • *www.divinacommedia.com*

8 Drinking at the Hemingway Pub, Como
It's debatable whether "Papa" actually drank atop the plush benches of this curious little bar tucked away near the port, but the cocktails are named after his books. ◈ *Via Juvara 16* • *031-271-631* • *www.pub/hemingway.com*

9 Going to Scarlet, Como
On Thursdays you can have dinner and dance the night away; on Saturdays there are often live bands and an interesting crowd. ◈ *Via Piadeni 24* • *031-305-555*

10 Enjoying the Lido Giardino, Menaggio
In the daytime, you can enjoy the private beach and pool. On Saturday nights, the banquet hall turns into a dance club that spills out into lakeside gardens. ◈ *Via Roma 11* • *0344-32-007* • *www.lidogiardino.com*

Price Categories

For a three-course	
meal for one with half	€ under €20
a bottle of wine (or	€€ €20–€30
equivalent meal), taxes	€€€ €30–€40
and extra charges.	€€€€ €40–€50
	€€€€€ over €50

Barchetta, Bellagio

🔟 Places to Eat

1 Le Sette Porte, Como
Highly original cuisine (strawberry risotto, chicken in orange-peppercorn sauce). The décor mixes rough stone and wrought-iron fixtures with funky modern elegance. ◉ *Via A Diaz 52a • 031-267-939 • Closed Sun • €€€€*

2 Ristorante Sociale, Como
One of the best-value set menus on the lake draws a local post-theatre crowd, Como's soccer team and budget-minded travellers alike. ◉ *Via Maestri Comacini 8 • 031-264-042 • Closed Tue • €€€*

3 Barchetta, Bellagio
For such a beloved resort, Bellagio oddly lacks superlative eateries, save perhaps this "little boat". The recipes are local and well-prepared, the ambience amicable and the prices appropriate. ◉ *Salita Mella 13 • 031-951-389 • Closed Oct–Mar • €€€€*

4 Nicolin, Lecco
Garden seating, a homely atmosphere and gourmet set-priced menus make this a foodie haven in the village of Maggianico outside Lecco. ◉ *Via Ponchielli 54 • 0341-422-122 • Closed Tue • €€€€€*

5 Crotto dei Platani, Brienno
A mix of rustic and elegant at a restaurant set in the remains of a castle. Charming candlelit terrace tables and regional food prepared with an inventive touch. ◉ *Via Regina 73 • 031-814-038 • Closed Mon & Wed lunch, Tue • €€€€€*

6 Vecchia Varenna, Varenna
The most romantic restaurant on the lake offers excellent fish dinners and dishes such as spinach tagliatelle in vegetable *ragù*. ◉ *Contrada Scoscesa 10 • 0341-830-793 • Closed Mon & Jan • €€€€€*

7 Locanda dell'Isola Comacina, Ossuccio
This island eatery's fixed-price feast has remained unaltered since 1947: antipasto, trout, fried chicken, cheese, fruit, *gelato*, water, wine and brandy-spiked coffee. ◉ *Isola Comacina • 0344-55-083 • www.comacina.it/isola • No credit cards • Closed Nov–Feb, Tue in spring • €€€€€*

8 Ostello La Primula, Menaggio
This hostel is a favourite spot for cheap dining. You serve yourself (and do your own washing up), but the cooking is pretty good. ◉ *Via IV Novembre 106 • 0344-32-356 • www.menaggiohostel.com • No credit cards • Open mid-Mar–early Nov • €*

9 Vecchia Menaggio, Menaggio
Many restaurants in town serve over-priced tourist slop, so locals patronize this homely trattoria and pizzeria. ◉ *Via al Lago 13 • 0344-32-082 • Closed Tue • €€€€*

10 Trattoria S Stefano, Lenno
The place for large portions of lake fish and pasta. For a great view, sit at a solarium table. ◉ *Piazza XI Febbraio 3 • 0344-55-434 • Closed Mon • €€€*

 Note: Unless otherwise stated, all restaurants accept credit cards and serve vegetarian meals

Price Categories

For a standard,	€ under €110
double room per	€€ €110–€160
night (with breakfast	€€€ €160–€210
if included), taxes	€€€€ €210–€270
and extra charges.	€€€€€ over €270

Left **Grand Hotel Menaggio** Right **Villa Cipressi, Varenna**

🔟 Places to Stay

1 Le Due Corti, Como

This ancient, rambling post house at the city's medieval walls has been a classy and atmospheric hotel since 1992. Excellent restaurant and popular bar, too. ◈ *Piazza Vittoria 12/13 • 031-328-111 • hotelduecorti@virgilio.it • Closed Nov–Feb • €€€*

2 Villa Flori, Como

Originally built in 1860 as a wedding gift for the owner's daughter and Italian hero Garibaldi. A genteel 19th-century air still clings to the rooms. ◈ *Via Cernobbio 12 • 031-33-820 • www.hotel villaflori.com • Closed Dec–Feb • €€€€*

3 Grand Hotel Villa Serbelloni, Bellagio

Bellagio's most elegant summer villa was transformed into a hotel in 1873. Rooms are luxurious. The mini-apartments stay open year-round, as do the gym, beauty centre and indoor pool. ◈ *Via Roma/Piazza Mazzini • 031-950-216 • www.villa serbelloni.com • Closed Dec–Mar • €€€€€*

4 Du Lac, Bellagio

The friendliest family-run hotel in town happens to sit right on the lakeside piazza, with lovely views from charming rooms fitted with antiques. ◈ *Piazza Mazzini 32 • 031-950-320 • www.bellagiohoteldulac.com • Closed mid-Nov–Easter • €€*

5 Suisse, Bellagio

Ten simple rooms with TVs and fancy wood furniture above a restaurant. ◈ *Piazza Mazzini 23 • 031-950-335 • www.bellagio.co.nz/suisse • Closed Dec–Feb • No A/C • €€*

6 Villa d'Este, Cernobbio

This sumptuous Renaissance villa is consistently rated among the top 10 hotels in the world and has long attracted royalty and celebrity. No expense is spared (antiques and silks, marbles and mahoganies), as reflected in the bill. ◈ *Cernobbio • 031-3481 • www.villa deste.it • Closed mid-Nov–Feb • €€€€€*

7 Milano, Varenna

This beloved old *pensione* may be turned into a boutique hotel in years to come. ◈ *Via XX Settembre 29 • 0341-830-298 • www.varenna. net • No A/C • Closed Nov–Mar • €€*

8 Villa Cipressi, Varenna

Rooms in this 16th-century villa *(see p109)* are spacious, with killer views – remarkable for the price. ◈ *Via IV Novembre 18 • 0341-830-113 • www.hotelvillacipressi.it • Limited A/C • Closed Nov–Mar • €€*

9 Grand Hotel Menaggio

This 19th-century villa retains a Belle Époque air, but rooms are modern. ◈ *Via IV Novembre 93 • 0344-30-640 • www.grandhotelmenaggio.com • Closed Nov–Jan • €€€*

10 Grand Hotel Tremezzo

The gardens of this 1910 hotel are worthy of neighbouring Villa Carlotta. The opulence extends to the highly impressive rooms. ◈ *Via Regina 8 • 0344-42-491 • www.grandhotel tremezzo.com • Closed Nov–Feb • €€€€*

 Note: *Unless otherwise stated, all hotels accept credit cards and have A/C (air conditioning) and en-suite bathrooms*

Left **Il Vittoriale, Gardone Riviera** Centre **Torri del Benaco** Right **The road to Castello di Arco**

Lake Garda

GARDA IS THE MOST SPORTING *of the Italian lakes. The crosswinds to the north and the dominating slopes of Monte Baldo draw windsurfers and paragliders, while other adrenaline-filled sports, such as rock climbing, and the more leisurely pursuit of golf, provide further distractions. Garda also enjoys some of the best Roman-era remains in northern Italy at Sirmione*

and Desenzano, as well as atmospheric medieval castles in Torri del Benaco, Malcesine, Valeggio and Sirmione. Since the 18th century, Garda's summer villas and verdant gardens have lured such luminaries as Goethe, Malcesine, Byron and D H Lawrence, though the region also found infamy as the place of Mussolini's last stand.

**Botanico Hruska,
Gardone Riviera**

🔟 Sights

1️⃣ Giardino Sigurtà

2️⃣ Gardaland

3️⃣ Grotte di Catullo, Sirmione

4️⃣ Rocca Scaligera, Sirmione

5️⃣ Villa Romana, Desenzano

6️⃣ Isola di Garda

7️⃣ Il Vittoriale, Gardone Riviera

8️⃣ Giardino Botanico Hruska, Gardone Riviera

9️⃣ Torri del Benaco

🔟 Castello di Arco, near Riva

Previous pages **Vineyards at Lake Lugano**

Giardino Sigurtà

1 Giardino Sigurtà
Carlo Sigurtà spent 40 years irrigating and planting this barren hillside in order to turn it into one of Italy's great gardens, with manicured lawns and pathways amid vibrant flower beds and reflecting pools. Hidden along the far western edge are some large enclosures where deer and goats run free. The gardens are a 20-minute drive south of the lakeside. ◎ *Outside Valeggio • Map G5 • 045-637-1033 • www.sigurta.it • Mar–Nov: 9am–6pm daily • Adm*

2 Gardaland
Under the icon of a goofy green dragon named Prezzemolo ("Parsley"), the park boasts roller coasters and carnival rides, a water park, jungle safari, ice shows, dolphin tricks and medieval spectacles. Italy's greatest theme park isn't quite Disneyland, but it's a hoot for the kids. ◎ *On the shore road, north of Peschiera • Map G4 • 045-644-9777 • www.gardaland.it • Closed Nov–Mar (except Christmas–New Year) • Adm*

3 Grotte di Catullo, Sirmione
Though the ancient Roman poet Catullus did take his holidays at Sirmione, there's no evidence to suggest that this vast, ancient house at the very tip of Sirmione's peninsula was actually his villa – in fact, it was probably built after Catullus's death, sometime in the 1st century BC. It is the best surviving example of a Roman private home in northern Italy, but this didn't stop it being misnamed a "grotto", the result of the romantically overgrown and cave-like state it had assumed by the Middle Ages. ◎ *Via Catullo • Map G4 • 030-916-157 • 8:30am–7pm Tue–Sun mid-Oct–Mar • Adm*

4 Rocca Scaligera, Sirmione
The 13th-century keep is at the narrowest point of Sirmione's long, thin peninsula. The striking, angular pale grey stone citadel, in use as a fortress until the 19th century, still dominates and protects the town – the only way to enter Sirmione is over the moat on one of the castle drawbridges, then under one of its squat gate towers. It's worth climbing the 30-m (95-ft) tower for the grand panorama. ◎ *Piazza Castello • Map G4 • 030-916-468 • 8:30am–7pm Tue–Sun • Adm*

Gardaland entrance

Il Vittoriale, Gardone Riviera

Gabriele d'Annunzio, one of Italy's most flamboyant characters from the turn of the 20th century *(see p45)*. ◈ Map G4 • 0365-296-511 • www.vittoriale.it • Apr–Sep: 8:30am–8pm Tue–Sun; Oct–Mar: 9am–5pm Tue–Sun • Adm

8 Giardino Botanico Hruska, Gardone Riviera

This small but lovely set of botanical gardens features more than 2,000 species on a terraced hillside *(see p45)*. ◈ Gardone Riviera • Tourist info: IAT Gardone, 0365-203-47 • 15 Mar–15 Oct: 9am–6pm daily • Adm

5 Villa Romana, Desenzano

The most important late Imperial villa remaining in Northern Italy was built in the 1st century BC, but the excellent polychrome floor mosaics are mostly of the 4th and 5th centuries. By that time, the local Romans were Christianized, which explains the late 4th-century glass bowl engraved with an image of Christ. ◈ Via Crocefisso 22 • Map G4 • 030-914-3547 • 9am–7pm Tue–Sun (to 5pm mid-Oct–Feb) • Adm

6 Isola di Garda

Garda's largest island once supported a monastery that attracted the great medieval saints: Francis of Assisi, Anthony of Padua and Bernardino of Siena. The monastery was destroyed by Napoleon and replaced in 1890–1903 with a Neo-Gothic Venetian-style villa and luxuriant English and Italianate gardens. Two-hour tours take place twice a week and, though the admission price is high, it does include a boat ride and a snack. ◈ Boats from Barbarano • Map G4 • 0365-62-294 • www.isoladelgarda.com • May–6 Oct: Tue & Thu at 9:40am • Adm (book in advance)

7 Il Vittoriale, Gardone Riviera

This over-the-top villa was built by poet, solider and adventurer

9 Torri del Benaco

This little town was once the capital of Lake Garda and important enough in the 14th century for Verona's Scaligeri family (who controlled much of Lake Garda) to build one of their castles. This one contains a modest museum on local history including the prehistoric rock carvings found on the

Giardino Botanico Hruska

Castello di Arco

nearby mountainsides. To see some of these 8,000-year-old etchings, follow signs off the main road up to Crer then walk up the trail about 15 minutes to a spot where the mountain's rock face shows through the undergrowth. ◈ *Map G4 • Castle: Viale Fratelli Lavanda 2 • Apr–May: 9:30am–12:30pm; Jun–Sep: 9:30am–1pm, 4:30–7:30pm; Oct: 9:30am–12:30pm, 2:30–6pm • Adm*

10 Castello di Arco, near Riva

Perched above town, this 12th-century castle is in a state of near-total ruin. Only one wall remains of the imposing central keep, and the sole room in the complex to survive intact was filled with debris until 1986. When it was cleared, a surprise discovery found several excellent late 14th-century frescoes depicting nobles playing at board games and war. ◈ *Arco • Map H2 • Apr–Sep: 10am–6pm; Mar & Oct: 10am–4pm; Nov–Feb 10am–3pm daily • Adm*

Lakeside Battles

In the 13th–15th centuries Venice vied with Milan for control of Lombardy *(see p32)*. The town of Torbole *(p120)* at the northern end of Lake Garda was the scene of a historic Milanese victory in 1439. Venice was caught while trying to smuggle supplies to the besieged town of Brescia – 26 ships had been sailed up the Adige River and dragged overland via Torbole into the lake when discovered.

Two Days on Lake Garda

Day One

🕐 If you're here to relax and sightsee rather than thrash the waves up near **Riva** *(see p120)*, then spend your days on the southern end of the lake. **Sirmione** *(p120)* is both a charming and lively base.

On your first day, stop in **Desenzano** *(p120)* to see the **Villa Romana** before driving out to Sirmione itself. Walk out to the far tip of the peninsula to wander the ruins of the **Grotte di Catullo** *(p117)*. On your way back into town, divert to the right to pop into San Pietro and see its medieval frescoes.

Navigate the throngs of the tiny centre to clamber up the balustrades of the **Rocca Scagliera** *(p117)* for a sunset panorama.

Take a *passeggiata* (stroll) with the crowds before heading down to the **Vecchia Lugana** *(p122)* for an exquisite evening meal.

Day Two

On day two, drive around to **Gardone Riviera** *(p120)* to tour Gabriele d'Annunzio's delightfully idiosyncratic **Il Vittoriale**, then have a refined meal on the terrace of the **Villa Fiordaliso** *(p122)*.

After lunch, take the time to wander the grounds at **Giardino Botanico Hruska** before either making your leisurely way back to Sirmione – if you are basing yourself there – or heading further up the lake to explore the small lakeside towns of **Limone** or **Riva** *(p120)*.

Left **Riva del Garda** Centre **Malcesine** Right **Torbole**

Lakeside Towns

1 Sirmione
The loveliest town on the lake is set at the tip of a long peninsula. It has the ruins of an ancient Roman villa and a remarkably intact medieval castle *(see p117)*.
🕾 *Map G4 • Tourist info: Viale Marconi 2 (just before town entrance) • 030-916-114 • www.comune.sirmione.bs.it*

2 Desenzano
A large and delightful town, settled in the Bronze Age and a retreat since the Roman era. Its top attraction is the Villa Romana *(see p118)*. 🕾 *Map G4 • Tourist info: Via Porto Vecchio 34 • 030-914-1510*

3 Salò
This gentelely faded resort became the capital of Mussolini's short-lived Republic of Salò (1943–5) in the closing chapters of World War II. 🕾 *Map G4 • Tourist info: Lungolago Zanardelli (in the Palazzo Comunale) • 0365-21-423*

4 Gardone Riviera
The fruits of Gardone's long popularity as a resort developed into magnificent villas and gardens, including Hruska and the Vittoriale *(see p118)*. 🕾 *Map G4 • Tourist info: Corso Repubblica 8 • 0365-20-347*

5 Toscolano–Maderno
These twin towns enjoy a great beach and the glorious church of Sant'Andrea, with its Romanesque capitals and fading frescoes. 🕾 *Map G4 • Tourist info: Lungolago Zanardelli 18 • 0365-641-330*

6 Limone sul Garda
Little Limone is tucked into a cove, with a long beach, small harbour and dozens of hotels.
🕾 *Map G3 • Tourist info: Lungolago Zanardelli 18, Maderno • 0365-641-330 • www.limone.com*

7 Riva del Garda
A bustling town, blessed with good surfing and the medieval Torre d'Apponale and Rocca Castle. Just inland lies Arco, home to a ruined castle *(see p119)*. 🕾 *Map H3 • Tourist info: Largo Medaglie d'Oro • 0464-554-444 • www.gardatrentino.com*

8 Torbole
History put Torbole on the map in 1439 *(see box on p119)*. Aside from that, the town is known chiefly as a good base for lake sports. 🕾 *Map H3 • Tourist info: Via Lungolago Verona 19 • 0464-505-177*

9 Malcesine
Among exhibitions on local natural history and prehistory, the town's castle contains a room devoted to Goethe, who was briefly imprisoned as a spy when he was caught sketching the castle. 🕾 *Map H3 • Open in high season • Tourist info: Via Capitanato 6–8 • 0457-400-044*

10 Bardolino
Bardolino has been famous since Roman times for its light red wine, celebrated at the museum. The town also has two wonderful Romanesque churches. 🕾 *Map G4 • Tourist info: P Aldo Moro • 045-721-0078 • Museo del Vino: www.museodelvino.it*

Browse www.bresciaholiday.com, www.gardatrentino.com and www.garda.com for more about Garda's lakeside towns

Left **Windsurfing** Centre **Lakeside swimming** Right **Rock climbing**

TOP 10 Things to Do

1 Windsurfing
Each summer, windsurfers from across Europe descend on Garda's wind-pounded northern shores – especially in Riva and Torbole – for some of the best lake surfing on the continent. Surf hire shops can be found in Riva, Torbole and Sirmione.

2 Diving
While this isn't the tropics, the waters are clearer than you might expect. Subterranean surprises include an underwater Jesus near Riva. Equipment is available in various outlets.

3 Mountain-Biking
Whether you want to explore the flatlands to the south, tackle mountains rising sheer from the north shores, or simply wend along the lake itself, hire a bike to see Garda at a leisurely pace.

4 Climbing and Paragliding
For adventure sports such as climbing and canyoning, head to Arco, just north of Riva, for the Guide Alpine or Multi Sport Centre, which can also hook you up with a paragliding run, as can Paragliding Club in Malcesine. ⊗ *Guide Alpine, 0464-507-075, www.guidealpine arco.com • Multi Sport Centre, 0464-531-080, www.multisport3.com • Paragliding Club, 045-740-0152*

5 A Round of Golf
The golf at Garda isn't great, but if you want to break out the nine-iron, there are several courses on the southwest shore and one on the east shore. ⊗ *Garda Golf, Soiano del Lago, 0365-674-707 • Golf Bogliaco, Toscolano, 0365-643-006 • Ca' Degli Ulivi, Torri del Benaco, 045-627-9030*

6 Fura Club, Lonato
One of the best clubs in Italy, Fura is a visual experience – a screen surrounds the dance floor, so you can watch yourself dance. ⊗ *Map G4 • Via Lavagnone 13 • 030-913-0652 • www.fura.it*

7 Disco Bar Café Latino, Riva
This disco overlooks the harbour from giant picture windows. ⊗ *Map H3 • Via Monte Oro 14 • 0464-555-0785 • Fri–Sat*

8 Kursaal, Sirmione
A happy blend of retro disco and ballroom dance hall. ⊗ *Map G4 • Via S Martino della Battaglia, Lugana • 030-919-163*

9 Dehor, Lonato
This disco spins house and 70s–80s pop and funk in a refined, Mediterranean-style club two miles off the autostrada. Once a month there's a theme party night. ⊗ *Map G4 • Via Fornace dei Gorghi 2 • 030-991-9948 • Fri, Sat & Tue*

10 Sesto Senso Club, Desenzano
Popular nightclub with laser lights pouring over a pounding dance floor shaking to house music, pop and Europop. ⊗ *Map G4 • Via dal Molin 99 • 030-914-2684*

Left **Cavallino** Right **Gemma**

🔟 Places to Eat

1 Esplanade, Desenzano

Elegance, stupendous lake views from its terrace and a perfect balance of creative cuisine and traditional recipes. Fresh lake fish, delicious mountain cheeses and over 800 wines in the cellar – wonderful. 🕔 Via Lario 10 • Map G4 • 030-914-3361 • Closed Wed • €€€€€

2 Cavallino, Desenzano

Gianfranco and Ornella Dallai run this debonair restaurant, with recipes based around fresh lake fish and fowl. Banquet-like "tasting menus" and fabulous desserts. 🕔 Via Gherla 30 • Map G4 • 030-912-0217 • Closed Sun dinner and Mon • €€€€€

3 Villa Fiordaliso, Gardone Riviera

A gorgeous historic villa and hotel (see p123), serving impeccable food that revisits the formidable tradition of Italian cooking (see also p69). 🕔 Via Nanardelli 150 • Map G4 • 0365-20-158 • Closed Mon & Tue lunch • €€€€€

4 Il Girasole, Sirmione

An elegant restaurant in the historic centre serving Italian food with an innovative twist. In summer you can eat alfresco on the flower-filled terrace. 🕔 Via Vittorio Emanuele 72 • Map G4 • 030-919-182 • Closed Wed lunch and Thu • €€€€€

5 La Rucola, Sirmione

The Bignotti family's genteel restaurant delights gourmands with a creative menu based around seasonal ingredients and local fish and meats. 🕔 Via Strentelle 3 • Map G4 • 030-916-326 • Closed Fri lunch and Thu • €€€€€

6 Vecchia Malcesine, Malcesine

Up on the panoramic terrace overlooking the town, you can enjoy lake specialities and cool breezes. 🕔 Via Pisort 6 • Map H3 • 045-740-0469 • Closed Wed • €€€€€

7 Gemma, Limone

A modest, friendly trattoria serving simple pastas and grilled fish. 🕔 Piazza Garibaldi 12 • Map G3 • 0365-954-014 • Closed Wed; Dec–Feb • €€€€

8 Birreria Spaten, Riva

Riva's Tyrolean roots show in this "Austrian" Bierhalle, where wurstel (sausage) and schnitzels hold sway on the menu. 🕔 Via Maffei 7 • Map H3 • 0464-553-670 • Closed Wed • €€€

9 Bella Napoli, Riva

A Sicilian couple has run this crowded joint for over 30 years, but they stick to a Neapolitan recipe for their wood-oven pizzas. 🕔 Via Diaz 29 • Map H3 • 0464-552-139 • Closed Wed • €€

10 Gardesana, Torri del Benaco

Book ahead for a table on this palace's long terrace overlooking the harbour. A highly praised mix of regional and international cooking. 🕔 Piazza Calderini 20 • Map G4 • 045-722-5411 • €€€€

Note: Unless otherwise stated, all restaurants accept credit cards and serve vegetarian meals

Price Categories

For a standard,	€ under €110
double room per	€€ €110–€160
night (with breakfast	€€€ €160–€210
if included), taxes	€€€€ €210–€270
and extra charges.	€€€€€ over €270

Left **Grand Hotel Fasano** Right **Sole**

Places to Stay

1 Park Hotel, Desenzano

A modest hotel with sort of modern-rustic décor and rooms overlooking the water. ◎ *Lungolago Cesare Battisti 17 • Map G4 • 030-914-3494 • www.parkhotelonline.it • €€*

2 Villa Fiordaliso, Gardone Riviera

Stay in the suite where Mussolini and his mistress hid out in their last weeks, then dine on the lakeside terrace *(see p122)*. ◎ *Via Zanardelli 150 • Map G4 • 0365-20-158 • www.villafiordaliso.it • €€€€*

3 Grand Hotel Fasano, Gardone Riviera

A Grand Dame of a hotel, spread along a lakeside garden of palms and willows. For extra privacy, book the Villa Principe, a former hunting lodge. ◎ *Gardone Riviera • Map G4 • 0365-290-220 • www.grand-hotel-fasano.it • Closed Nov–Mar • No credit cards • A/C in some rooms • €€€*

4 Park Hotel Villa Cortine, Sirmione

An exclusive Neo-Palladian stunner sitting on a panoramic perch above its own regal gardens and beach. Antique furnishings and exquisite dining. ◎ *Via Grotte 6 • Map G4 • 030-990-5890 • www.hotelvillacortine.com • Closed 21 Oct–27 Mar • €€€€€*

5 Grifone, Sirmione

A delightful budget hotel that's fairly quiet and right on the lake with its own private beach. ◎ *Via Bocchio 4 • Map G4 • 030-916-014 • No credit cards • No A/C • €*

6 Sole, Riva del Garda

One of the best hotels in Riva: lakeside piazza location; decent restaurant; great value; and free bicycles for guests. ◎ *Piazza 3 Novembre 35 • Map H3 • 0464-552-686 • www.hotelsole.net • Closed Nov–mid-Mar • A/C in some rooms • €*

7 Hotel Du Lac et Du Park, Riva del Garda

A luxurious retreat, with a fitness and beauty centre, a small park of tiny lakes, pools, tennis courts and mini-golf, and a gorgeous private sandy beach. ◎ *Viale Rovereto 44 • Map H3 • 0464-566-600 • www.hoteldulac-riva.it • €€*

8 Le Palme, Limone sul Garda

Venetian-style rooms, most overlooking the lake, and a small pool in gardens that are shaded by lemon trees. ◎ *Via Porto 36 • Map G3 • 0365-954-681 • www.sanhotels.it • Closed Nov–Easter • €*

9 Malcesine, Malcesine

The town's oldest hotel sits on the little port square – ask for a room overlooking the water. The low prices also include half-board. ◎ *Piazza Pallone 4 • Map H3 • 045-740-0173 • No A/C • Closed Nov–Mar • €*

10 Romantik Hotel Laurin, Salò

A canary-yellow 1905 villa with exquisite detailing, spacious high-ceilinged rooms and a tiny garden pool. ◎ *Viale Landi 9 • Map G4 • 0365-223-82 • www.laurinsalo.com • €€€€*

Note: Unless otherwise stated, all hotels accept credit cards and have A/C (air conditioning) and en-suite bathrooms

Left **Piazza del Comune, Cremona** Centre **Da Candida, Lake Lugano** Right **Leoncino Rossi, Mantova**

Smaller Lakes and Towns

WHILE IT IS TRUE THAT THE LAKES OF *Maggiore, Como and Garda* are the best-developed and most obvious tourist destinations of the region, offering a wide range of accommodation and watersports facilities, do not overlook the lesser-known lakes and towns of Lombardy. The museums of Bergamo, Mantova and others may not be as important as Milan's, the villas less grand than Como's, but a few days spent off the beaten path can offer a rewarding break from the crowds that throng Milan's great sights and back up traffic for hours along the Big Three lakes.

🔟 Sights

1. Lake Orta
2. Lake Varese
3. Lake Lugano
4. Bergamo
5. Lake Iseo
6. Lake Idro
7. Brescia
8. Mantova
9. Sabbioneta
10. Cremona

Mantova

Lake Orta

This is the region's western-most lake, and its main town – with a traffic-free, medieval centre – is Orta San Giulio. The wooded promontory on which it stands was turned into a *Sacro Monte*, a path lined by 20 decorated chapels, between 1591 and 1770. Boats sail from here to the tiny idyll of Isola San Giulio. At the north end of Lake Orta, Omegna is the unlikely centre of Italian industrial design. Its craft factories founded at the beginning of the 20th century developed into the giants of housewares, such as Alessi and Bialetti *(see also p58)*. The Forum Museum celebrates this utilitarian art form. ✪ *Map A3 • Tourist info: Via Panoramica in Orta S Giulio, 0322-905-614; www.distrettolaghi.it • Forum Museum: Omegna; www.forumomegna.org; adm*

Lake Varese

Varese is part of a quartet of small lakes (along with Monate, Comábbio and pond-sized Biandronno) that were popular with 18th-century Lombard landscape painters for their bucolic settings, Romanesque churches, mirror-like waters and Alpine backdrops. A few factories notwithstanding, the area is largely unchanged today. Roads rarely touch the lake shores, forcing detours into lakeside villages. This marshy region has yielded some important prehis-

Lake Lugano

toric finds, most especially on Lake Varese's Isolino islet (catch a boat from Biandronno, June–September), though the actual finds are kept at the Musei Civici in Varese town. ✪ *Map B3 • Tourist info: Via C Carrobbio 2, Varese • 0332-283-604*

Lake Lugano

Lake Lugano snakes between Italy and Switzerland, and its principal resort, Campione d'Italia, is in fact an Italian enclave within Switzerland's borders. Campione is a slightly raucous island of pizza restaurants and gambling casinos interrupting the more staid Swiss shoreline, where to the south, outside Melide, is the delightfully kitsch Swiss Miniatur, with its vaguely accurate "map" of Switzerland, including all its major monuments reproduced at 1/25 of their actual size. ✪ *Map B2–C2 • Tourist info: Campione d'Italia, Via Volta 3; www.campioneitalia.com • Swiss Miniatur, Nr Melide; www.swissminiatur.ch; adm*

Lake Varese

Piazza Vecchia, Bergamo

4 Bergamo

A vibrant city of medieval streets, fashionable boutiques and Renaissance churches, Bergamo is one of the Top 10 of the region *(see pp26–7)*. ✎ *Map D3*

5 Lake Iseo

This is the prettiest of the smaller lakes, and the town of Iseo itself – with modest hotel complexes and watersports facilities – is as touristy as it gets. Further north, at Lovere, Galleria Taldini has a small collection of paintings by the likes of Jacopo Bellini, Tintoretto and Tiepolo. The interior of the church of Santa Maria della Neve, on the edge of Pisogne, is a visual delight of equal merit, its abundant frescoes painted by Romanino in 1532–4 (if the church is locked, enquire at the café inside the adjacent cloisters). ✎ *Map E3–4 • Tourist info: Via Marconi 26, Iseo, 030-980-209, www.lagoiseo.com • Galleria Taldini, Lovere, Map F3; Apr–Oct: Tue–Sun; adm*

6 Lake Idro

This slip of a lake just west of Garda is renowned for its trout, sailing, windsurfing and skiing in the surrounding mountains. Sports and the lake's natural beauty are to the fore, while cultural highlights are Anfo's 16th-century castle and the 15th-century frescos in the church of Sant'Antonio. ✎ *Map G3 • Tourist info: Via Trento 15, Idro, 0365-83-224*

7 Brescia

The industrialized face of Brescia hides a fine medieval and Renaissance centre, with several mementos of its time as a Roman colony (including a temple and theatre). Installed in the ancient San Salvatore e Santa Giulia monastery is the excellent Museo della Città, a repository of prehistoric, Roman and medieval objects and artworks. The painting gallery (Pinacoteca Tosio-Matinengo) sports works by local Renaissance artists as well as the great Raphael and Tintoretto. ✎ *Map F4 • Tourist info: Via Musei 32, 030-374-9916; www.provincia.brescia.it • Museo della Città, Via dei Musei; adm*

8 Mantova

The palaces, churches and artworks by Mantegna and Giulio Romano help make Mantova, too, one of the entire region's Top 10 *(see pp28–9)*. ✎ *Map H6*

Left **Lake Iseo** Right **Piazza del Comune, Cremona**

Mantova

9 Sabbioneta

Duke Vespasiano Gonzaga had this town built from scratch in the late 16th century, the closest any potentate ever got to fully realizing the ideal Renaissance city. A single ticket lets you in to all the major sights: Palazzo del Giardino (the summer palace); the fabulous trompe-l'oeil frescoed Galleria; and the Teatro all'Antica, the first purpose-built theatre since antiquity. ⊗ Map G6 • Tourist info: Piazza d'Armi 1 • 0375-221-044 • www.comune. sabbioneta.mn.it

10 Cremona

This town has been home to some of the world's finest ever makers of stringed instruments, a craft that reached its pinnacle in the 17th century at the workshop of Antonio Stradivari. It is hardly surprising, then, that Cremona's top sights are fiddle-oriented: the Raccolta dei Violini is a roomful of exquisite 17th- and 18th-century instruments; while Museo Stradivariano pulls out all the big names in violin-making (Amati, Stradivarius, Guaneri). ⊗ Map E6 • Tourist info: Piazza del Comune 5 • 0372-23-233 • www.aptcremona.it

Two Days from Garda to Como

Day One

🕐 The smaller lakes and towns are scattered across Lombardy and eastern Piemonte, impossible to see in one short trip, but some of the best can been enjoyed on a leisurely two-day drive from Lake Garda to Lake Como.

Head west on the A4 Autostrada to **Brescia** to spend your first morning admiring its museum and Roman sights. Having lunched at **Due Stelle** (see p129), continue to nearby **Lake Iseo**. Explore the eastern shore, especially the Romanino frescoes in Pisogne, the small museum in Lovere and the weird rock pinnacles outside of Zone.

If you can, spend the night at **I Due Roccoli** (see p148), or at least have dinner there (p129).

Day Two

On Day Two, drive north into the **Val Calmonica** (see p47) to view some of the valley's prehistoric rock carvings. Then head back south to diverge west at Lovere for the back road to **Bergamo**.

Check into your hotel and spend the afternoon enjoying the Renaissance architecture and carvings of the Colleoni Chapel, the excellent Accademia Carrara gallery, medieval town square and, of course, the town's shops, cafés and wine bars.

End your day with a hearty meal at the aptly named **Antica Hosteria del Vino Buono** (the "Ancient Inn of Good Wine"; see p129).

Left **I Portici del Comune** Right **Oblò pub sign**

Shops, Cafés and Nightspots

1 Lagostina, Crusinallo-Omegna, Lake Orta

The discount factory outlet for the famed homewares designer. Get 30–50% off here and at similar outlets on the same road – Bialetti (No. 106) and Fratelli Piazza Effepi (No. 242) – and Alessi (Via privata Alessi). Look for slight irregulars *(sformati)* for bigger savings. 🖎 *Map A3 • Via IV Novembre 39*

2 Armani Factory Store, Vertemate

Well worth a visit, especially for the massive discounts (30–50%) on men's and women's clothing. 🖎 *Map D3–4 • Strada Provinciale per Bergamo • 031-887-373*

3 Vineria Cozzi, Bergamo

Old-fashioned wine bar with glass cases and a marble cutting board in the front, and a more private back room and tiny, plant-filled courtyard to the side. Dabble with a little wine tasting of your own and some splendid little snacks *(see also p65).* 🖎 *Map D3 • Via Colleoni 22 • 035-238-836 • €€€*

4 Caffè del Tasso, Bergamo

This historic café on the main piazza has been a local living room (and site of rebellious debates) since the 16th century. 🖎 *Map D3 • Piazza Vecchia 3 • 035-237-966 • €*

5 Papageno Pub, Bergamo

Little round tables and Guinness on tap just a few steps off the main square. 🖎 *Map D3 • Via Colleoni 1b • 035-236-624*

6 Lubiam, Mantova

One of Italy's top men's tailors since 1911. This warehouse outlet holds a staggering array of choices (over 1,000 suits, 1,500 jackets etc) at 35% off the usual prices. 🖎 *Map H6 • Viale Fiume 55*

7 Oblò, Mantova

Popular pub with friendly proprietors, good beers, great *panini*, a non-smoking room and a loyal local clientele. The music is loud, but it's not a raucous place. 🖎 *Map H6 • Via Arrivabene 50*

8 Sperlari, Cremona

Wood-floored shop from 1836 selling its own sweets, *torrone* (nougat), cordials, liqueurs, candied fruits and "cherries with spirit". 🖎 *Map E6 • Via Solferino 25*

9 Concerts and Opera at Fondazione Teatro Ponchielli, Cremona

Fancy hearing a string quartet composed entirely of Stradivarius instruments? Cremona's Teatro Ponchielli is about the only place in the world where this happens regularly. 🖎 *Map E6 • Corso V Emanuele 52 • www.teatro ponchielli.it*

10 I Portici del Comune, Cremona

Good coffee, *gelato* (ice cream) and *panini*. Tables ranged under an arcade across the piazza from the prettiest Duomo façade in Lombardy. 🖎 *Map E6 • Piazza del Comune 2 • €*

Price Categories

For a three-course meal for one with half a bottle of wine (or equivalent meal), taxes and extra charges.	€ under €20
	€€ €20–€30
	€€€ €30–€40
	€€€€ €40–€50
	€€€€€ over €50

Left **Da Candida** Right **I Due Roccoli**

🔟 Places to Eat

1 I Due Roccoli, Iseo, Lake Iseo

The restaurant of an excellent hotel *(see p148)* set high above the town of Iseo. Refined regional food is served on a patio overlooking lawns and woods *(see also p69)*. ◈ Map C4 • Via Silvio Bonomelli • 030-982-2977 • Closed Nov–mid-Mar • €€€€€

2 Da Candida, Campione d'Italia, Lake Lugano

Elegant restaurant mixing French and Italian cuisine, famed for its homemade fois gras and polenta slow-cooked over the dining room's open fireplace. ◈ Map C2 • Via Marco 4 • 0041-649-7541 • Closed Sun & Mon lunch • €€€€€

3 Antica Agnello, Lake Orta

Cosy taverna serving lake fish, local game and creative regional dishes. Always the freshest ingredients. ◈ Map A3 • Via Olina 18 • 0322-90-259 • Closed Tue • €€€

4 Villa Crespi, Lake Orta

Stylish restaurant in a unique Moorish-fantasy hotel *(see p148)*. Elegant service and top-quality regional cuisine. ◈ Map A3 • Via Fava 18 • 0322-911-908 • www.lagodortahotels.com • €€€

5 Antica Hosteria del Vino Buono, Bergamo

Hearty bergamasco fare and some good tasting menus in the simple rooms of a wedge-shaped medieval *palazzo*. ◈ Map D3 • Via Donizetti 25 • 035-247-993 • Closed Mon • €€€

6 Taverna del Colleoni & del Angelo, Bergamo

Formal restaurant installed in an evocative Renaissance *palazzo* on the main piazza, with outdoor dining in summer. Turn to the back of the menu for local specialities. ◈ Map D3 • Piazza Vecchia 7 • 035-232-596 • Closed Mon • €€€€€

7 Leoncino Rosso, Mantova

A rustic restaurant just off the main square that has been serving scrumptious mantovana fare since 1750, such as *tortelli di zucca* (pasta stuffed with pumpkin). ◈ Map H6 • Via Giustiziati 33 • 0376-323-277 • Closed Sun dinner • €€

8 Ochina Bianca, Mantova

Distinctive variations on local dishes and a judicious use of lake fish. ◈ Map H6 • Via Finzi 2 • 0376-323-700 • Closed Mon • €€€

9 La Sosta, Cremona

A wood-panelled osteria loved by locals for its home cooking. The *gnocchi vecchia Cremona* (honey-roasted potato dumplings stuffed with salami) is a 17th-century recipe. ◈ Map E6 • Via Sicardo 9 • 0372-456-656 • Closed Mon and dinner Sun • €€€€

10 Due Stelle, Brescia

Satisfying foodies for over a century with local cuisine and a choice of settings: around a 16th-century courtyard fountain or by the fireplace inside. ◈ Map F4 • Via S Faustino 48 • 030-42-370 • Closed Mon, Sun pm • €€€€€

STREETSMART

Arriving in Milan
132

Getting Around
Milan and the Lakes
133

General Information
134

Ways to Save Money
135

Banking and
Communications
136

Shopping Tips
137

Health and Safety Tips
138

Things to Avoid
139

Travellers with Special
Concerns
140

Tips for Families
141

Tips for Eating Out
142

Accommodation Tips
143

Places to Stay
144–149

MILAN AND THE LAKES

Left **Coach services at Malpensa Airport** Centre **Linate Airport** Right **Arriving by car**

🔟 Arriving in Milan

1 By Air from the UK

Alitalia, British Airways, Ryanair, Easyjet and British Midlands all fly direct London to Milan; bmibaby flies East Midlands to Milan. British Midlands also flies into Bergamo. From Ireland, Aer Lingus flies direct Dublin to Milan; British Airways and Alitalia route you through London.

2 By Air from North America

There are direct flights to Milan from the major North American cities on most US and Canadian airlines as well as Italy's Alitalia. Most arrive at Malpensa airport.

3 By Air from Australia

Alitalia flies Sydney to Rome, from where you can transfer to Milan. Qantas flies from various Australian and New Zealand cities to Rome via Bangkok, though it's cheaper to fly via London.

4 By Air from the Continent

The national airlines of each European nation connect to Milan. On the continent, Ryanair flies to Milan from Frankfurt-Hahn, Brussels, Paris and Barcelona; Virgin Express flies in from Brussels.

5 Internet Air Bargains

Most airlines use their websites to promote sales and bargain tickets. Expedia and Travelocity collate most regular best fares offered from the US and UK. Booking engines run by airline consortiums include Orbitz in the US and Opodo in Europe. Also check sites such as Lastminute.com.

6 Malpensa Airport

Closer to Como than to Milan, the airport is linked by the Malpensa Express to Cadorna station in western Milan (40 mins, leaving every half hour). You can also catch a bus: Malpensa Express or Shuttle (50 mins, 2–3 per hour) to central Milan.

7 Linate Airport

Milan's secondary airport, just east of the city, receives many Alitalia flights as well as those from across Europe. STAM and ATM buses leave every half hour for the 25-minute trip to central Milan (buy tickets on bus). Alternatively, take a taxi into the centre. It's the quickest and easiest option, and not terribly expensive.

8 By Train

From London, you can take the Eurostar to Paris and pick up one of three daily trains to Milan (they take between 6 hours 30 mins and 10 hours 30 mins). Various express trains (EC/IC/EN) head to Milan from many other European cities.

9 Milan's Train Stations

Most trains arrive at Milan's Stazione Centrale; its tourist office is hidden down a corridor of shops off the arrivals hall. Other stations include Cadorna, also known as Milano Nord (services to Malpensa airport and Como), Porta Genova (Asti, Alessandra and other points southwest), and Porta Garibaldi (Lecco).

10 By Car

The A4 comes into Italy via southern France, passing Turin on its way to Milan; it continues to Venice. The only way in from the north is over one of the Alpine passes: the Sempione from the Geneva region; St Gotthard from Luzern, or St Bernard from the Swiss/German border. They link up in Italy as the A2.

Directory

Airline Websites
www.alitalia.it
www.ba.com
www.ryanair.com
www.flybmi.com
www.bmibaby.com
www.easyjet.com
www.aerlingus.ie
www.qantas.com
www.virginexpress.com

Internet Agents
www.expedia.co.uk
www.travelocity.co.uk
www.opodo.co.uk

Milan's Airports
• 02-7485-2200 • www.
sea-aeroportimilano.it

Left **Coach tour** Centre **Road sign** Right **Ferry**

Getting Around Milan & the Lakes

1 By Train
Italian trains, run by FS, are speedy and efficient, but don't cover every Lombard corner. Each station posts its own schedule – departures on yellow, arrivals on white – and newsstands sell national schedules. Ticket lines can be long (automated machines are now helping), and strikes (*sciopero*) annoyingly frequent. You must stamp one end of your ticket at the station's or track's yellow box before boarding.

2 By Coach (Long-Distance Bus)
Coaches (pullman) are slower and no cheaper than trains. They are best used to reach destinations where trains don't go.

3 By Ferry
Lakes Como, Garda, Maggiore and Iseo each have a public ferry system run by Navigazione Laghi. The smaller lakes have skiffs connecting towns or running out to islands. Private boats and water taxis charge at least twice as much as public boats.

4 By Rental Car
The best way to explore the environs. Local outfits are rarely cheaper than international agents, and arranging a rental from your home country is invariably the best option. Most companies require a theft protection charge, but check if your credit card covers this first.

5 Road Signs and Maps
TCI (Touring Club Italiano) maps are best and widely available in Italy. Michelin maps have more sightseeing indications, including scenic roads highlighted in green. Italian road signs (green for routing via Autostrada highways, blue for state roads) indicate destinations more often than route numbers; on any road, check the map to note the towns and villages it passes, as well as the destination city.

6 Road Rules
Speed limits: 30–50 kmh (20–30 mph) in town; 80–110 kmh (50–70 mph) on two-lane roads; and 130 kmh (80 mph) on highways. Left lanes are truly for passing only. On wide, hard-shouldered roads, Italians regularly pass by swerving into the road, which obliges oncoming traffic to use its own hard shoulder.

7 Tolls and Fuel
Lombardy's only toll roads are the autostrade connecting the main cities. Unleaded petrol is *senza piombo* or *verde*; diesel is *gasolio*. Though most stations close Sundays, many have automated machines that accept notes and credit cards.

8 Parking
Though few hotels have their own parking, many have agreements with local garages. Round blue signs with a red slash mean no parking. Legal parking is always marked: white-lined spaces are free; yellow-lined spaces are restricted to residents only and blue spaces available for an hourly fee.

9 City Bus, Tram and Metro
Milan has a mix of transport: buses, trams and an underground, and all use the same tickets. Buy them at tobacconists (*tabacchi*, indicated by a white-on-brown "T" sign), newsstands, or bars. Stamp one end on the bus or tram when you board. They are good for a set time period during which you may transfer.

10 Taxis
You'll find taxi ranks at airports and stations. Any hotel or restaurant will know the local Radio Taxi number to call for you. Standard rates go up with luggage, after 8pm, on Sundays, and for trips outside the centre. Tip about 10 per cent.

Directory

Trains
www.trenitalia.com

Ferries
www.navigazionelaghi.it

Car Rentals
www.europebycar.com
www.autoeurope.com

For leasing a car over a period of more than three weeks see p135

Left **Tourist Board** Centre **Shopping arcade** Right **Newsagent**

🔟 General Information

1 Italian State Tourism Board

Provincial tourism boards control most information, so ENIT (Ente Nazionale Italiano per il Turismo), the national tourist office, is well-intentioned but of little help. However, you will find links to the local Lombardy tourist boards on their website.

2 Tourist Offices in Lombardy

Local *informazioni turistiche* offices, often indicated as "IAT" or "Pro Loco", are good for free maps, sight and museum opening hours, and hotel directories. The amount of information beyond that varies widely, but most are friendly. Milan's tourist office is on Piazza del Duomo at Via Marconi 1 (02-7252-4301), with a branch in Stazione Centrale (02-7252-4360).

3 Immigration Laws

Citizens of the UK, Ireland, US, Canada, New Zealand and Australia need only a valid passport to visit Italy for up to 90 days for tourism.

4 Customs

You may bring into Italy personal items with the following quirky limits: 400 cigarettes (or 550 grammes of tobacco), 2 cameras, 10 rolls of film, a pair of skis, two tennis rackets, one shooting gun with 200 cartridges and a litre of alcohol.

5 Opening Hours

Most shops and businesses open at 8 or 9am, shut for *riposo* from about 12:30 to 3 or 4pm (museums and churches, too), and close around 6–8pm. In larger cities, the *riposo* is disappearing in favour of *orario continuato*, working straight through.

6 Electricity and Outlets

Italy is on 220V/50 cycles. To operate a 110V device you need a converter (most laptops and camcorders have this built in). To plug it in, you need an adapter from your pronged plugs to Continental Europe's two round pins.

7 TV & Newspapers

Most hotels 3-stars and above get satellite TV with CNN and BBC news. Train station and central piazza newsstands are best for finding English-language newspapers (the *International Herald Tribune* comes with an *Italy Daily* insert). *Informer* (www.informer.it) is Milan's ex-pat English-language magazine.

8 When to Go

Lombardy has a mild climate, a bit hotter and drier than most of the UK. August heat can be oppressive, while January snow is common. Spring's middle ground keeps hotels booked in the cities, but summer is the season for the lakes. There is some winter skiing in the Alps ringing the lakes to the north.

9 High Season and Holidays

High season is Easter–Jul and Sep–Oct. But while cities are deserted mid to late Aug, lakeside resorts are packed right through Jul–Aug. Milan's trade fairs (Mar, Apr, Oct) make finding hotel rooms and classier dinner reservations nigh impossible. National holidays are: 1 & 6 Jan, Easter Sun & Mon, 25 Apr, 1 May, 15 Aug, 1 Nov, and 8, 25 & 26 Dec.

10 What to Pack

Italians dress well, so it's a good idea to take at least one nice outfit, though few restaurants require jacket and tie. Many churches do not allow bare knees or shoulders (no shorts, miniskirts, or vests).

Tourism Websites

• *Italian Tourist Board: www.enit.it*

• *Lombardy: www. regione.lombardia.it*

• *Piemonte: www.regi one.piemonte.it/turismo*

• *Milan: www.milano infotourist.com*

• *Garda: www.garda world.com*

• *Como: www.lake como.org*

• *Maggiore: www. distrettodeilaghi.it*

Left **Sightseers** Centre **One-star hotel** Right **Local craft stall**

🔟 Ways to Save Money

1 Sightseeing for Free
Lombardy's churches are free, and contain some of Italy's greatest art and architecture. The best chapels often require some payment, however. Italy's gorgeous, *palazzo*-rimmed squares are free theatres of life, and the price of a cappuccino will get you a front row seat.

2 Sightseeing at a Discount
Discount admission to sights and museums varies greatly: the age cut-off may be 6, 12, 14, or 18, or just "students" and seniors (over 60 or sometimes 65). National museums are free under 18 and over 60 to everyone except US citizens. Many towns now sell tickets that combine several sights.

3 Travel Discounts
Under 18s can buy a Carta Verde for about €13 and receive 30 per cent discount on any train ticket; the same deal for over 60s is called Carta Argento. But none of Italy's rail passes will pay off financially if you're sticking just to Lombardy.

4 Lease a Car
For periods longer than 21 days, a short-term lease is often cheaper than renting a car. Unlike with rentals, you also get full insurance coverage with no deductable, plus a brand-new car straight from the factory. The pioneers in this arrangement are Europe By Car and Auto Europe (see p133), though other agencies are starting to pick up on the concept.

5 Save Money on Accommodation
Generally, prices rise the closer you are to the centre of town. Making do with a one or two-star hotel or taking a room without private bathroom in a central hotel is preferable to looking outside the centre or in the uninteresting but cheap train station neighbourhood. Also, avoid using the room phone and mini-bar – both are overpriced.

6 Cheap Eats
In food-loving Italy, price or category of restaurant has little to do with the quality of food, so a cheaper *osteria* or trattoria can be as tasty an option as a fancy *ristorante*. Be aware that appetizers tend to cost almost as much as first courses, but tap water (*acqua dal rubinetto*) is usually free. *Tavole calde* and bars (see p142) offer super cheap hot meals.

7 Have a Picnic
For little money, you can visit a string of small delis (*alimentari*), green-grocers (*fruttivendolo*), bread and pastry shops (*panetteria/pasticceria*), and wine stores (*enoteca/fiaschetteria*) and create your own picnic fit for a king. Then choose your location – overlooking a lake, or in a town's main square, perhaps.

8 Pay in Cash
Cash will often get you a discount in shops and smaller hotels, as they won't have to pay a credit card commission. However, make sure you leave with some kind of receipt, as by law you have to carry it 400 m beyond the store (a whole branch of the Italian police is devoted to financial fraud).

9 Visit in the Off-Season
Spring and now autumn too are getting more crowded than summer, and hotels and airlines often extend their high-season prices accordingly. Mid-Nov to just before Easter is low season in Italy, when rates on air fares and hotels can drop considerably. However, facilities around the lakes (especially in resort towns) almost completely shut down in winter.

10 Shop Wisely
When possible, non-EU visitors should save purchasing for one store to hurdle the VAT limit and get a refund (see p137). Go for artisan products rather than souvenirs, and, if you can, purchase directly from the crafts-people. Also, buy what you can't get at home – look for local produce.

Left **ATM sign** Centre **Telephone Kiosks** Right **Internet Café**

Banking and Communications

1 Exchanging Money

If you can't use an ATM to get cash, change money at a bank (or, for American Express card-holders, an Amex office) for the next-best rates and lowest charges. Take your passport as ID. "Cambio" exchange booths are open longer, but have worse rates. Shops and hotels generally offer poor rates for traveller's cheques.

2 ATMs

The fastest, easiest and cheapest way to get local currency is via an ATM *(bancomat)*, drawing money directly from your home current account (savings accounts are not so easily accessed).

3 Credit Cards

MasterCard and Visa are the most widely accepted – just about everywhere except the smallest family-run shops, trattorie and hotels. American Express is also accepted in many places. You can get credit card cash advances from ATMs, but, unlike with purchases, interest usually starts accruing immediately.

4 Traveller's Cheques

While still the safest way to carry money, traveller's cheques are doomed by the evolution of easier and cheaper ATMs. However, a few cheques are good for

emergencies. Buy them denominated in euros. Note that personal cheques are useless, except for Amex card-holders, who can cash cheques at American Express offices.

5 Currency

Italy has joined most of Continental Europe in adopting the Euro (€), which replaced the lira. Euro coins come in €1 and €2, and in 1, 2, 5, 10, 20, and 50 euro cents. Bills come in €5, €10, €20, €50, €100, €200, and €500.

6 Public Phones

Most pay phones in Italy now accept only pre-paid phone cards *(scheda telefonica)* you can buy in several denominations at tobacconists *(tabacchi)* and newsstands. Break off the corner before inserting it. There is also a range of pre-paid *carta telefonica internazionale* that give you a number to call and a code for international calls.

7 Calling Home

Arranging to take a call in your hotel room is invariably cheaper than using the Italian phone system. But if you want to make an outward call, use the cards described above or international phone booths in major post offices. To reverse charges, dial the international operator at 170. Calls can usually be placed at

hotels, but the charges are excessive. To call Italy from abroad, dial your international prefix (011 in the US, 00 in most other countries), then Italy's country code of 39, followed by the number, including that initial zero (which, formerly, was dropped).

8 Internet Access

Internet cafés are forever popping up, frequently disappearing with equal alacrity (ask at the tourist office if you don't stumble upon any). Increasingly, hotels offer internet access too.

9 Postal Service

To send postcards and letters, just ask any tobacconist *(tabacchi)* or newsagent for stamps *(francobolli)* for the country to which you are mailing. Then drop the post in the slot of the mail box (usually red) labelled "*per tutte le altre destinazioni*" (not "*per la città*").

10 Receiving Mail

Mail addressed to "[Your Name] / Fermo Posta / [Town Name], Italia / ITALY" should make it to the main local post office (though it helps to add the postal code, if you can find it). There's a small fee to pick it up, though Amex card-holders can receive free of charge letters sent to "[Your Name] / Client Mail / American Express / Via Brera 3 / 20121 Milano, Italia / ITALY".

Left **Shopping street** Centre **Bottles of Chianti** Right **Local ceramic craft**

🔟 Shopping Tips

1 Shop Hours
Shops open around 8am and close 7–8pm, with long afternoon breaks *(see p134)*.

2 Haggling
Bartering over price is the life-blood of markets, but isn't the norm in the majority of shops. Many market stallholders now hail from Middle Eastern countries where bargaining is an art form, so be ready to go through the full ritual: you acting less and less interested, the stallholder acting more and more offended.

3 Tax Refunds
Italy's Value Added Tax (IVA) is included in the price tag of every item. Non-EU visitors who spend more than €155 in one shop can get the tax refunded. Ask the store to help you fill in the forms; then bring them and the receipts to the customs office at the airport to complete the paperwork. Your refund will be mailed (though it may take some months). Stores marked "Tax Free Shopping for Tourists" speed up the process, giving you a cheque for the customs office to stamp, which can then be redeemed at the airport's Tax Free Shopping desk.

4 Customs Limits
UK and Irish citizens can bring home virtually anything duty free (though, in principle, limits such as no more than 90 litres of wine apply). US citizens are limited to $400 worth of goods duty-free, including 1 litre of alcohol, 200 cigarettes and 100 cigars. Canadian, Australian, and New Zealand limitations are roughly similar. Unless you are from the EU, you are not allowed to take home flowers, bulbs, fruits, vegetables, meats (unless tinned) and cheeses runnier than brie.

5 Fashion
One of the world's elite capitals of fashion, Milan is home to many top names in haute couture: Prada, Armani, Versace, Mila Schön, Krizia, Missoni and Ferré, to name but a few. In March and October, supermodels draped in next season's fashions parade the runways in the MODIT fashion shows. Top couture isn't likely to be any cheaper in Milan (unless you go to a discount outlet), but buying clothes here has a certain cachet.

6 Design Objects
Italians are masters of industrial design, from Ferraris to funky Alessi tea kettles. So if the Ferrari doesn't fit your budget, consider some elegant or quirky kitchenware instead.

7 Bargain Hunting
For craftware, such as ceramics, carved wood and even leather shoes, try to visit the workshops and buy at source. For everything else, use the Italian shopper's three cardinal "S"s: *sconti* (reduced prices), *saldi* (sales), and *spacci* (discount outlets).

8 Ship Your Souvenirs
Rather than carry your perhaps bulky purchases all around Lombardy, see if the shop can ship them home for you on the spot. The fee is often worth the hassle saved. If you have a rental car big enough to store your goods, you could try the other tack: at the end of your trip post home your dirty laundry and anything you won't miss for a while, then use the space saved to pack your souvenirs.

9 Wine
Italy's best souvenir, though rather heavy (and US citizens can only take home one bottle without paying a duty). Shipping is expensive, so save it for when you discover a small vineyard whose wines aren't exported and buy a whole case.

10 Crafts
Italy is renowned for the quality of its hand-painted ceramics – souvenirs that have a practical use as well as an aesthetic appeal. Milan is also home to fine jewellers, from big names such as Bulgari to artisans labouring in small boutiques.

Left **Ambulance** Centre **Farmacia sign** Right **Trams**

🔟 Health and Safety Tips

1 Emergencies
You can dial 113 for general emergencies: see the Directory for more specific numbers. Note that the car breakdown number is a pay towing service.

2 Safety
Italians do tend to drive aggressively, so be attentive behind the wheel. Also, take steps to avoid pickpockets *(see below)*. Women (especially young foreign women) may be pestered, but it's mostly harmless. Apart from these things, Italy is a remarkably safe country, and violent crime is rare.

3 Pickpockets
On crowded trams and buses, the metro, and around train stations and other areas where tourists congregate, pickpockets will be at work. Keep your wits about you and ensure your passport, credit cards, plane tickets and money are well hidden.

4 Street Beggars
Every European city has its street beggars and master pickpockets, and Milan is no exception. Begging varies from the apathetic seated figure with a tin for change to the confrontational and occasionally aggressive street-hardened homeless person. A common pickpocketing technique is to use distraction, such as crowding you or using a cardboard sign to disguise the act of thievery. But, despite this, begging and street crime are not especially rife in Milan.

5 Scams
While not particularly rampant, scams are sometimes attempted on the most clueless-seeming of tourists. Taxis might try to set the meter for "out of town" rates rather than local. Restaurants might try to pad the bill with items not ordered, and are the mostly likely to try and double-charge your credit card. Just be attentive, and the unscrupulous are unlikely to try.

6 The Police
There are two main police branches: the regular Polizia and the military-trained national Carabinieri force. A police office is called a *questura*.

7 Medical Charges
It's sensible to take out medical insurance, even if your country has a reciprocal agreement with Italy. Usually you must pay any hospital charges up front and apply for reimbursement when you get home. US Blue Cross/Blue Shield members can visit affiliated hospitals in Italy, using their card as at home.

8 Italian Hospitals
Italian hospitals *(ospedale)* are efficient and semi-privatized. The emergency room is called *pronto soccorso*. Unless you're admitted overnight, they'll usually give you a check-up, write a prescription and send you off with a smile, no paperwork involved.

9 Pharmacies
Italian *farmacie* are usually well equipped and excellent in helping with minor ailments. They take turns to stay open at night and on Sunday – the information will be posted on the window. Otherwise, head for the 24-hour pharmacy in Milan's Stazione Centrale train station.

10 Food and Water Safety
Italian water is safe to drink everywhere except on trains and any source signposted *"aqua non potabile."* Food is largely safe, though uncooked seafood is always risky.

Directory

Emergency Numbers
• *General 113*
• *Ambulance 118*
• *Fire 115*
• *Car breakdown 116*

Police
• *Regular Polizia 113*
• *Carabinieri 112*

Blue Cross
www.bluecross.com

24-hour Pharmacy
Stazione Centrale, Milan • 02-669-0935

Left **Hôtel des Iles Borromées, Lake Maggiore** Centre **Cheap fashion** Right **Central Milan traffic**

Things to Avoid

1 Milan in August
August in Milan is often brutally hot, and almost the whole city goes on holiday, including many pharmacists and grocers. The only bit of town open for business is the Navigli and its glut of restaurants and bars, but fair warning: bring plenty of insect repellant.

2 The Lakes in Winter
Most hotels shut down from October or November through to February, many reopening only at Easter. Only Lake Maggiore keeps a longer season, with many of its inns and restaurants closing only for December or January.

3 Not Booking a Milan Hotel During Trade Fairs
The usual tourist seasons don't apply to business-orientated Milan. The months to watch out for are March, April and October when major trade fairs and fashion shows keep even the most basic, one-star hotels booked solid. Even outside these months, it can be difficult to find a room. It's always wise to book ahead.

4 Full Pension Hotel Rates
Hotels on the lakes often cater largely to habitual holidaymakers who stay a week or more and rarely budge from their chosen tanning spots. The package deals they try to force on clients reflect this; some require stays of three nights, many insist you take at least a half-board deal. Try to negotiate more leeway.

5 Driving in Milan
A car is utterly unnecessary in Milan: some roads are now pedestrianized; when it is available, parking is limited and expensive; and to the uninitiated, Italians seem to drive like maniacs. Car hire makes sense only for touring around the lakes.

6 Not Reserving Tickets for the Last Supper
If you do not book ahead to visit Leonardo's *Last Supper (see pp8–9)*, you will be turned away at the door. Try to reserve as far in advance as possible. This is not an exaggeration.

7 Overloading Your Itinerary
It might make sense to visit Milan's museums and monuments back-to-back, but once you get up to the lakes, it is time to take it easy. Enjoy the Italian art of *dolce far niente*, the "sweetness of doing nothing".

8 Boutique Price Tags
Window shopping amid the renowned boutiques of Milan's Quadrilatero d'Oro can be fun, but few visitors really have deep enough pockets to turn browsing into a new wardrobe. Luckily, this epicentre of high fashion has also spawned a thriving business of *spacci* (stock houses) where you can get last year's fashions, slight irregulars and odd sizes at 30% to 50% off the usual price tags *(see also p137)*. Sometimes you even come across a "used" dress that was worn just once by a model on a Milanese catwalk.

9 Wearing a Waist Pack
Despite being sold on its seeming convenience for the luggage-laden traveller, the waist pack is arguably the worst travel accessory ever invented. It places all of your most important belongings at the perfect height for a light-fingered thief to rifle through at his or her leisure.

10 Gardaland Without Children
Though Gardaland may be Italy's best theme park and deserving of a recommendation in this book as a top attraction for kids *(see pp63 & 117)*, bear in mind that Italy isn't renowned for its theme parks. So while it is vaunted as one of Lake Garda's largest individual "sights", it isn't worthwhile unless you have bored children in tow or you love all things kitsch.

Left **Student travellers** Right **Senior visitors**

🔟 Travellers with Special Concerns

1 Tips for Students

Milan has a vast student population, many of whom hang out in the bars of the Navigli district, and in clubs just north of there in Ticinese. They're also habitués of the bars in the Brera neighbourhood. To get discounts when sightseeing, ask for a "studente".

2 Resources for Students

Remember to take your ISIC (International Student Identity Card), the only card widely accepted as proof of status.

3 Tips for the Elderly

Discounts for *anziani* ("ancient ones") are often available at sights and on transport *(see p135)*.

4 Resources for the Elderly

Besides books and magazines devoted to the mature traveller, you can get good travel information, advice on tour operators, and sometimes discounts, from the major national associations for retired persons, such as ARP (UK) and AARP (US).

5 Tips for Women

The "Latin Lover" is alive and well, and women may receive more attention than they are used to, or happy with. Open staring, verbal come-ons, even bottom-pinching and the like are not uncommon. Be firm, to stop such behaviour in its tracks.

6 Resources for Women

There is little in the way of official resources for women, other than a few clubs for ex-pats and visitors: the Benvenuto Club for social activities, and the PWA (Professional Women's Association), for career networking.

7 Tips for the Disabled

Preservation laws deter owners from altering the city's older buildings in order to accommodate wheelchairs. However, most major museums have disabled access, and many hotels (especially 4- and 5-star properties) have created a few wheelchair-friendly rooms. Most Metro stops are wheelchair accessible, but restaurant toilets may not be – check first.

8 Resources for the Disabled

RADAR (the Royal Association for Disability and Rehabilitation) in London publishes a series of useful pamphlets. Join Holiday Care Service, in Surrey, for advice on disabled-friendly accommodation.

9 Tips for Gay and Lesbian Travellers

Homosexuality is broadly accepted in as cosmopolitan a city as Milan, which hosted the World Pride festival in 2000. Moderate physical affection will draw little undue attention.

10 Resources for Gays & Lesbians

Italy's national organization for homosexuals (curiously, a subset of the National Communist Youth Alliance) is ARCI-Gay; the lesbian branch is ARCI-Lesbica. Milan's gay bookshop is Libreria Babele; there are gay travel guides put out by Ferrari, Spartacus and Frommer's. Useful websites include www.gay.it and www.geocities.com/arcobalenoMI.

Directory

Students
- STA Travel 0870 1 600 599; www.statravel.co.uk
- Council Travel www.counciltravel.com
- Travel CUTS www.travelcuts.com

Seniors
- ARP 020 8764 3344 www.arp.org.uk
- AARP 800-424-3410 www.aarp.org

Women
- www.pwa-milan.org

Disabled
- RADAR 020 7250 3222, www.radar.org.uk
- Holiday Care Service 01293 774 535

Gay/Lesbian
- ARCI-Gay 02-5412-2225 www.arcigaymilano.org
- ARCI-Lesbica 02-2901-4027 www.women.it/arciles
- Libreria Babele, Via S Nicolao 10

Left **Sightseeing tour** Right **Station concourse**

≋ Tips for Families

1 Try Picnicking
It saves money, makes for a fun outing, gives children a chance to pick out what they want from the wonderful delis and bakers, and also gives them a break from all those restaurants where they have to be on best behaviour – though this is, in fact, less of an issue in Italy. Also, since travelling with children slows you down in many ways, picnic lunches (always quicker than sitting down to a three-course meal) help make up some lost time.

2 Order Half-Portions
A *mezza porzione* for smaller appetites costs 30–50 per cent less than a full portion. Adults feeling weighed down by all this great Italian food, who yet feel compelled to continue trying it all can cash in on this tip as well as children.

3 Share a Room
Rather than booking two separate rooms for parents and kids, trade some privacy for savings and bunk the whole clan in one room. Each extra bed costs no more than 35 per cent extra on the price of a double; cots and baby cribs are even less. But if some time apart is the only route to familial peace, ask if the hotel has any family suites or rooms that share a common door.

4 Make a Home-Base
Try to stay in one hotel or apartment if possible, and make day-trips rather than moving on from one town to the next. The constant upheaval can be exhausting for kids, changing hotels is time-consuming and rates for stays of three days or longer are usually reduced.

5 Sightseeing Discounts
Ridotto is the word for reduced-price tickets, which may apply to all students or at least the under 18s. A few sights offer a *biglietto famiglia* for family group discount. Admission may be free under the age of 6, 12 or even 18 (especially for citizens of the EU).

6 Train Discounts
Those under 27 can buy a Carta Verde from train stations to save 20 per cent on tickets.

7 Rent a Car
Renting one mid-sized car is far cheaper than four or even three sets of train tickets, and has the added benefit of allowing you more flexibility in terms of itinerary and speed *(see p133)*.

8 Gelato Breaks
Don't over-pack your itinerary. Skip a few museums, and reduce the number of "boring old gardens" you plan to visit. Take time to enjoy some delicious Italian ice cream instead.

9 Use Riposo Wisely
Sightseeing is exhausting. Therefore, do as the Italians do, and take a *riposo* (a nap) after lunch rather than trying to pack still more sights into your holiday schedule.

10 Enjoy Italy's family culture
Italy's is a multigenerational culture, accustomed to welcoming large family groups all travelling together. And a visiting child attempting to speak a little Italian can be a great icebreaker.

Gelateria

Left **Formal dinner placings** Centre **A friendly waiter** Right **Dishes at a tavola calda**

Tips for Eating Out

Restaurant Types
1 A ristorante is the most formal, expensive, eatery; a trattoria a family-run, moderately-priced joint; an *osteria* anything from a simple trattoria to the equivalent of a pub with dishes of cured meats and cheeses.

The Italian Meal
2 Italian meals, especially dinners, are drawn-out affairs of two to four hours, with the courses listed below followed by an espresso and digestive liqueur *(digestivo)* such as grappa. Lunch is similar and was once the day's largest meal; but life's modern pace is shortening it. Breakfast is traditionally an espresso or cappuccino with a sweetened roll or croissant *(brioche* or *cornetto)*.

Antipasto
3 This is the appetizer course. A typical offering would be bruschetta (toasted bread rubbed with garlic, olive oil, salt, and sometimes tomatoes) and/or cured meats such as prosciutto, salami, bresaola (thin slices of dried beef) and carpaccio (wafer-thin raw beef). Also popular are *nervetti* (a cold salad of pickled calf tendons) or a caprese salad of tomatoes and mozzarella.

Primo
4 The first course. Risotto (creamy arborio rice) is usually studded with seasonal vegetables, sausage bits *(alla mantovana)*, or sometimes a seafood medley. Pastas include *tortelli di zucca* (pumpkin-stuffed pockets), *strangolapreti* (balls of ricotta and spinach), *agnolotti* (tiny, meat-filled ravioli), and *pizzoccheri* (a casserole of buckwheat pasta layered with cheese, potatoes and onions). Soups *(minestre)* include minestrone (vegetable soup), simple *zuppa pavese* (bread and eggs in broth), and *cassoeüla* (see p66).

Secondo
5 The main course. Meats include *bistecca* or *manzo* (beef), *vitello* (veal), *agnello/abbacchio* (mutton/spring lamb), *pollo* (chicken), *maiale* (pork), *cinghiale* (boar), *coniglio* (rabbit), and *anatra* (duck). A *cotoletta* is a cutlet, usually veal; a *braciola* is a chop, usually pork. Meats are usually simply grilled or roasted. A *grigliata mista* is a hearty mixed meat platter. Lake fish are covered on p67.

Dolce
6 The dessert. Most popular are hard almond biscuits with sweet wine for dunking, lemon sorbet *(sorbetto)*, or *gelato* (ice cream). Egg custards are also favourites, as is *tiramisù* (a rich dessert with espresso and sweet cream). A *macedonia* is a diced fresh fruit cup.

Wine and Water
7 No Italian meal is complete without red *(rosso)* or white *(bianco)* wine *(vino)*; either a carafe *(un litro)* or a half-carafe *(mezzo litro)* of the usually excellent house wine *(vino della casa)*, or a bottle of the good stuff. Italians temper their wine by drinking equal amounts of water, either fizzy *(gassata, frizzante)* or still *(non-gassata)*.

Cover Charges and Tipping
8 The *pane e coperto* (bread and cover) charge of €1 to €4 per person is unavoidable. If the menu says *"servizio incluso"*, service charge is built in – though it is customary to round up the bill. If not, tip a discretionary 10 to 15 per cent.

Restaurant Etiquette
9 Jacket and tie are rarely required. Waiters expect you to linger over your meal, and won't rush you (some visitors mistake this for slow service).

Bars and Tavole Calde
10 Most Italian bars serve sandwiches and pastries alongside a morning cappuccino and *cornetto*, espresso throughout the day and apéritifs in the evening. A *tavola calda* is a glorified bar with pre-prepared dishes steaming in trays behind a glass counter.

Left **Hotel room** Centre **Camping site** Right **Hostel in Menaggio**

Accommodation Tips

1 Hotels
Italian hotels are categorized from one-star (basic) to five-stars (deluxe), based largely on the amenities offered rather than such esoteric considerations as charm, historic setting, or central location. At three stars and above, all rooms have at least private bathroom, TV and phone.

2 Agriturismi (Farm Stays)
Some working farms – usually vineyards – offer rooms. This translates to largely inexpensive lodgings in bucolic settings. Some are luxury, some very rustic. Agriturist, Terra Nostra and Turismo Verde are the main consortiums.

3 Villa Companies
Top villa rental agencies in the UK include International Chapters and Cottages to Castles. In the US, try Marjorie Shaw's Insider's Italy, the Parker Company and Villas International.

4 Choosing a Villa
Ask for a schematic layout and as many pictures as possible of the interior and exterior of the apartment/villa and the grounds. Find out how many others might share the villa or other houses on the complex.

5 Rooms to Rent
The tourist office has a list of these invariably cheap options. They can range from a lovely room with semi-private access to a cramped spare bedroom in someone's modern apartment. It can be a great way to meet locals.

6 Camping and Caravaning
Camp sites *(campeggi)* are widespread, but you end up paying almost as much as for a cheap hotel: a fee per person, for your vehicle and for the pitch itself *(see p149)*.

7 Hostels
All cities and major towns have cheap beds in sex-segregated, shared dorms. They are full of international students, and usually impose a curfew of midnight or so. Most official IYH hostels are on the edges of towns.

8 Should You Reserve?
Making a reservation in advance is always wise, especially for the first night of your stay and particularly if you have your heart set on a special hotel. The best-known can book up months in advance. However, if you are not fussy, you should be able to find a room when you arrive, at most times of year you visit.

9 Booking Services
For a small fee, most tourist offices and private hotel consortiums will help you find a room. Their offices are usually located in the main train stations and airports. So far, the countless internet booking services have highly erratic stables of hotels in their databases.

10 Quirks that can Affect the Price
Rooms without private bath, without a view, or for stays longer than three days often come cheaper. An extra bed in a room usually costs 30–35 per cent more. Breakfast may not be included; parking may be extra; and prices on minibar items and phone calls (local or international) are often exorbitant.

Directory

Agriturismi
• www.agriturist.it
• www.terranostra.it
• www.turismoverde.it

Villas
• International Chapters (020) 7722-0722, www.international chapters.com
• Cottages to Castles (01622) 775217, www. cottages-castles.com
• Marjorie Shaw's Insider's Italy www.insidersitaly.com
• The Parker Company (800) 280-2811, www. theparkercompany.com
• Villas International (800) 221-2260, www. villasintl.com

Hostels
• www.hiayh.org
• www.hostels.com
• www.ostelli.it

Left **Grand Hotel et de Milan** Right **Principe di Savoia**

Milan's Luxury Hotels

1 Four Seasons
The top hotel in town was converted in 1993 from a 15th-century convent, complete with some frescoes. Superior rooms are on the street side, deluxe ones open on to the cloisters. Milan's best shops are nearby, and one of the area's best restaurants, Il Teatro, is in the hotel's basement *(see p68).* ✪ *Via Gesù 8 • Map N2 • 02-796-976 • www.four seasons.com/milan • €€€€€*

2 Grand Hotel et de Milan
The Grand has been Milan's most intimate luxury hotel since 1863, a darling of inveterate shoppers and La Scala stars (it was Callas's Milan home). Composer Giuseppe Verdi was resident for 30 years. ✪ *Via Manzoni 29 • Map M3 • 02-723-141 • www.grandhotel etdemilan.it • €€€€€*

3 Park Hyatt Milan
This luxurious hotel is situated in the heart of the city, just steps from Piazza Duomo and the Scala opera house, and within easy access to Via Montenapoleone's shops. The Ed Tuttle-designed interior features Bang & Olufsen TVs, large marble bathrooms and walk-in closets. There is also a spa with a small fitness centre and two treatment rooms. ✪ *Via Tommaso Grossi 1 • Map L3 • 02-8821-1234 • www.milan. park.hyatt.com • €€€€€*

4 Hotel de la Ville
It's near the Duomo, and enjoys the facilities of any upmarket hotel, but at prices 20 to 40 per cent lower than the competition. The rooms are adorned with silk and 18th-century-style antiques. ✪ *Via Hoepli 6 • Map M3 • 02-867-651 • www.hotel delavillemilano.com • €€€€€*

5 Principe di Savoia
Built in 1927 in a 19th-century Lombard style, this is the most elegant of Milan's top hotels. Its Principe Tower was built in 2000 for businessmen who like their modern office conveniences in an old-fashioned atmosphere. ✪ *Piazza della Repubblica 17 • Map N1 • 02-62-301 • www.principedisavoia.com • €€€€€*

6 Spadari al Duomo
This gem, filled with original works by contemporary artists, is near Piazza Duomo. Stylish rooms include features such as marble sinks and hydromassage shower stalls. Room rates drop 20 per cent Friday to Sunday. ✪ *Via Spadari 11 • Map L4 • 02-7200-2371 • www. spadarihotel.com • €€€€*

7 Antica Locanda dei Mercanti
This converted apartment between the Duomo and Castello is a wonderful home-away-from-home. The quiet rooms have floral draperies, matching headboards and the occasional exposed beam. The more expensive *terrazzo* rooms have small terraces and canopy beds. There is also a small restaurant and bar. ✪ *Via San Tomaso 6 • Map L3 • 02-805-4080 • www.locanda.it • €€€*

8 Diana Majestic
A Liberty-style hotel focused on a lush courtyard garden. The rooms have a modern elegance with such top-end amenities as Bose stereos. ✪ *Viale Piave 42 • Map P2 • 02-20-581 • www. sheraton.com • €€€€€*

9 Ariosto Hotel
Luxurious amenities and refined service without a high price tag. Rooms either overlook the private garden or open on to the Liberty-style façades of this residential street, and all come with lovely wood furnishings, high-speed internet connections, and VCR. Free bikes are provided for guests. ✪ *Via Ariosto 22 • 02-481-7844 • www. brerahotels.com • €€€*

10 Carlton Hotel Baglioni
This 1962 hotel on the north side of the shopping district sports non-smoking rooms (unusual in Italy), 19th-century–style silk brocades and inlaid furnishings. There is also a business centre. ✪ *Via Senato 5 • Map N2 • 02-77-077 • www.baglioni hotels.com • €€€€€*

Price Categories

For a standard,	€ under €110
double room per	€€ €110–€160
night (with breakfast	€€€ €160–€210
if included), taxes	€€€€ €210–€270
and extra charges.	€€€€€ over €270

Excelsior Hotel Gallia

🔟 Milan's Best Business Hotels

1 Excelsior Hotel Gallia

This bastion of sophistication knits together the best of both worlds: genuine 1937 Liberty-style class with modern comforts and amenities. The rooms have a quirky elegance, the baths are marble-clad, and the dual phone lines have a PC hook-up. Ten conference rooms are so well-equipped there are even simultaneous translators. The solo business traveller will thrill at the extra-wide single beds – uncommon in Italy. ⦿ *Piazzale Duca d'Aosta 9* • *02-678-5713* • *www.lemeridien-excelsior hotelgallia.it* • *€€€€*

2 Westin Palace

The general décor is a genteel Empire style, but the "smart rooms" have high-tech facilities, and the plush business centre has on-staff translators. Choose from 13 well-equipped conference rooms. There is also a fully equipped gym. ⦿ *Piazza della Repubblica 20* • *Map N1* • *02-63-361* • *www.westin.com* • *€€€€€*

3 Una Hotel Century

Near the central station, north of Piazza della Repubblica, this property is made up entirely of business suites: 148 sleek, modern units, each with a bedroom and separate living room/office. ⦿ *Via F Filzi 25B* • *02-675-041* • *www.unahotel.it* • *€€€€€*

4 Capitol

This towering modern hotel boasts the latest in business technologies. Rooms include dual phone/modem lines, internet access via your TV, and in the suites (both executive and conference), a private PC, fax, and large screen TV. ⦿ *Via Cimarosa 6* • *02-438-591* • *www.capitol milano.com* • *€€€€*

5 Doriagrand Hotel

A large hotel with modern, comfortable bedrooms, four conference rooms, and secretarial services. Tourists will appreciate that weekend rates are a mere 40 per cent of the midweek prices. ⦿ *Viale Andrea Doria 22* • *02-6741-1411* • *www. adhotels.com* • *€€€€*

6 Una Hotel Cusani

In 2001 the Radisson Bonaparte became part of the Una hotel chain, but that hasn't changed its spacious rooms or comforts. A prime location, across from the Castello Sforzesco. ⦿ *Via Cusani 13* • *Map L3* • *02-85-601* • *www.una hotel.it* • *€€€€€*

7 Marriott

With 18 meeting rooms, a well-equipped business centre, a floor of Executive rooms, and a location straight down the street from the Fiera, the Milan Marriott was built for the business traveller. If only it were nearer the centre for some sightseeing when the meetings are over. ⦿ *Via Washington 66* • *02-48-521* • *www.marriott.com* • *€€€€*

8 Mediolanum

The austerity of this cement-grey hotel is relieved by the personal touch brought by family management, though many rooms are rather on the small side. Facilities include meeting rooms with secretarial services and ISDN lines. ⦿ *Via Mauro Macchi 1* • *02-670-5312* • *www.medio lanumhotel.com* • *€€€€*

9 Grand Hotel Fieramilano

If you're in town for a trade show, you can get no more convenient a hotel than this, opposite the Fiera. Contemporary rooms are given a touch of warmth by richly patterned fabrics. ⦿ *Viale S Boezio 20* • *02-336-221* • *www.atahotels.com* • *€€€€€*

10 Hotel Executive

This massive hotel on the north end of the Brera district has rooms decorated in a sumptuous antique style, masking its range of high-tech amenities. There's a full-fledged business centre and 21 meeting rooms. ⦿ *Viale Sturzo 45* • *02-62-941* • *www.hotel-executive. com* • *€€€€€*

Left **Rovello** Centre **Santa Marta** Right **Genius Hotel Downtown**

Milan's Mid-Range Hotels

1 Antica Locanda Solferino

Milan's most eccentric hotel is beloved by fashion gurus and film stars. What it lacks in amenities such as minibars and large bathrooms, it makes up for with its flower-fringed balconies, homey mismatched furnishings and breakfast-in-bed. ✆ *Via Castelfidardo 2 • Map M1 • 02-657-0129 • www.antica locandasolferino.it • €€€€*

2 London

The most old-fashioned of three hotels on a block near the Castello offers smiling service, bright, large rooms with worn but solid furnishings, and 10 per cent off the next-door restaurant. Rooms get smaller as you go up each floor, so try for the ground floor. ✆ *Via Rovello 3 • Map L3 • 02-7202-0166 • www.hotel londonmilano.com • €€€*

3 Rovello

The most characterful of the Via Rovello hotels has been renovated with shiny wood floors, stylish furnishings, and orthopaedic beds. But it has kept the wood-beamed ceilings, classy dressing rooms and unusually spacious bedrooms. ✆ *Via Rovello 18 • Map L3 • 02-8646-4654 • www. hotelrovello.it • €*

4 Giulio Cesare

The most modernized of the hotels on Via Rovello sports sleek new baths and contemporary furnishings lit by elegantly tall windows. Amenities, however, are a notch below those of its neighbours, with gruff staff and no laundry or concierge service. ✆ *Via Rovello 10 • Map L3 • 02-7200-3915 • www. giuliocesarehotel.it • €€*

5 Santa Marta

The Rovello's sister hotel sits on one of the few streets remaining of Old Milan; a crooked cobblestoned lane of little shops and classic Milanese restaurants. Sensible, comfortable rooms range from cramped to spacious. You're well positioned for Milan's top sights. ✆ *Via Santa Marta 4 • Map L4 • 02-804-567 • www.hotel-santamarta.it • €€€*

6 Ariston

A novel approach to Italian inn-keeping: an eco-hotel. The electrical devices are engineered for low power consumption; the showers conserve water; the tap water and even the air are purified; the breakfast spread is organic. Naturally, the desk rents out bicycles. ✆ *Largo Carrobbio 2 • Map K/L4 • 02-7200-0556 • www. brera hotels.com • €€€€*

7 Hotel Canada

Situated in the University quarter, the Canada appeals to both leisure and business travellers with its simple, streamlined rooms, all of which have en-suite bathrooms; the suites also have Jacuzzis. A panoramic terrace affords beautiful views over the city. ✆ *Via Santa Sofia 16 • Map M5 • 02-5830-4844 • www.canadahotel.it • €€*

8 Genius Hotel Downtown

A resort chain bought this modern hotel on a quiet street in 2002 and renovated it with bright, thick carpets, new furnishings and orthopaedic beds, and largish baths. There is an entire non-smoking floor. ✆ *Via Porlezza 4 • 02-7209-4644 • www.hotel genius.it • €€*

9 Hotel Star

This modern hotel sits on a quiet side-street between the hopping Brera neighbourhood and the Castello. The parquet floors with their Oriental rugs support orthopaedic beds and slightly worn, functional furnishings. The baths, however, are ultra-modern. ✆ *Via dei Bossi 5 • Map L3 • 02-801-501 • www.hotelstar.it • €€€*

10 Gran Duca di York

In the 19th century, this *palazzo* was used by the nearby cathedral to house visiting cardinals. Today, rooms are marred by ugly 1970s furnishings, yet it is comfortable, some bedrooms have terraces and the location is great. ✆ *Via Moneta 1a • Map L4 • 02-874-863 • www.ducadiyork.com • €€€€*

Note: Unless otherwise stated, all hotels on p146 accept credit cards and have en-suite bathrooms and A/C (air conditioning)

Price Categories

For a standard, double room per night (with breakfast if included), taxes and extra charges.

€ under €110
€€ €110–€160
€€€ €160–€210
€€€€ €210–€270
€€€€€ over €270

Left **Speronari** Right **Aliseo**

🔟 Milan's Budget Gems

1 Speronari
Two-star amenities (only half the rooms have private baths and TVs) and a four-star location on a pedestrian street one block off the Piazza del Duomo, all at one-star prices. Rooms on the top floors get more light; those on the courtyard escape the noise from trams. 🕲 *Via Speronari 4 • Map M4 • 02-8646-1125 • No A/C • €*

2 Hotel Sempione
This personable hotel, located halfway between the train station and Piazza Duomo, is close to the shopping and entertainment hub of Corso Buenos Aires. The airy and simple rooms offer all modern comforts. 🕲 *Via Finocchiaro Aprile 11 • Map M5 • 02-3656-8261 • www.hotelsempione.it • €*

3 Gritti
Blandly modern but friendly three-star place on a quiet piazza. The elderly owner is always around to keep an eye on things, and the location and amenities (A/C, minibar, TV) make it a steal. 🕲 *Piazza S Maria Beltrade 4 • 02-801-056 • www.hotelgritti.com • A/C • €€*

4 Paganini
Staying at this tiny hotel on a residential street off Corso Buenos Aires is like moving in with friends. The high-ceilinged rooms are large and kitted out with spare but homey furnishings. Only one of the eight rooms has a private bathroom. 🕲 *Via Paganini 6 • 02-204-7443 • €*

5 Aliseo
It may lack character and class, but the price is hard to beat anywhere in Milan, let alone just a few blocks south of the Duomo. None of the seven basic rooms has a private bathroom, but shared facilities are large, new and clean. 🕲 *Corso Italia 6 • Map L5 • 02-8058-1019 • €*

6 Kennedy
Of the many bare-bones *pensioni* in this neighbourhood near the public gardens and Corso Buenos Aires, the Kennedy singles itself out for cleanliness, friendliness and the fact that its fifth-floor location allows a few rooms to peek over the rooftops at the distant spires of the Duomo. For once, an espresso and croissant in the hotel bar is as cheap as at a local café. Two of the rooms have full bathrooms. 🕲 *Viale Tunisia 6 • Map P1 • 02-2940-0934 • www.kennedyhotel.it • €*

7 Nuovo
This modest one-star hotel is hidden two blocks behind the Duomo and has a few quirky touches, such as huge stone sinks, moulded door frames and stone balconies, but otherwise is fitted with beaten-up modular furnishings and prone to a grumpy management. 🕲 *Piazza Beccaria 6 • Map N4 • 02-8646-4444 • Fax 02-7200-1752 • €*

8 Commercio
A tiny hotel perfectly sited between the Brera, Castello and Duomo. It does most of its business with workmen, but tourists are welcome as long as they don't mind rooms with box showers, sink and bidet (but no toilet), and paying cash in advance. Ask to see several rooms as some are much nicer than others. 🕲 *Via Mercato 1/Via d. Erbe • Map L2 • 02-8646 3880 • No credit cards • €*

9 Vecchia Milano
It's on the high end of inexpensive, but worth it for the charming, semi-rustic wood panelling, good-sized rooms and location on a quiet street west of the Duomo. Many rooms come with third beds that flip down from the wall – great for budget-minded families. 🕲 *Via Borromei 4 • Map L4 • 02-875-042 • www.hotel vecchiamilano.it • €€*

10 Ostello Piero Rotta
Milan's rather institutional hostel is located out of the city centre, near the San Siro stadium. It has a nice garden, however. 🕲 *Via M Bassi 2 • 02-3926-7095 • www.lombardy hostels.it • €*

Left **Agnello d'Oro, Bergamo** Centre **Broletto, Mantova** Right **I Due Roccoli, Iseo**

Hotels in the Smaller Towns

1 San Lorenzo, Bergamo

The classiest hotel in Bergamo opened in 1998 in a converted convent at the north end of the atmospheric upper town. The service is impeccable, and the rooms done in a pleasing minimalist style. ◈ *Piazza Mascheroni 9a • Map D3 • 035-237-383 • www.hotelsanlorenzobg.it • €€*

2 Agnello d'Oro, Bergamo

Built in 1600, the hotel has a mountain chalet look to it. The receptionists can be brusque, but the rooms are cosy, if unimaginatively furnished. Book a room at the front, where small, flower-filled balconies give views over the bustling main drag below. ◈ *Via Gombito 22 • Map D3 • 035-249-883 • €*

3 San Lorenzo, Mantova

This lovely hotel is furnished with luxurious appointments and 18th- and 19th-century panache. It occupies a set of townhouses amid the pedestrianized historic district and has a roof terrace offering a panorama of Mantova. ◈ *Piazza Concordia 14 • Map H6 • 0376-220-500 • www. hotelsanlorenzo.it • €€€*

4 Broletto, Mantova
A 16th-century *palazzo* of wood-beamed ceilings and a vaguely rustic contemporary

décor sits a mere 100 m (300 ft) from Lake Inferiore. ◈ *Via Accademia 1 • Map H6 • 0376-326-784 • €€*

5 Hotel Impero, Cremona

The 53 rooms of this hotel are elegantly decorated, combining period furniture and modern facilities. Located in the town centre, the hotel offers views over the cathedral square and the town hall. ◈ *Piazza della Pace 21 • Map E6 • 0372-413-013 • www.hotelimpero.cr.it • €*

6 I Due Roccoli, Iseo
Set in its own quiet park high above the lake on the road to Polaveno, this family-run hotel offers a countryside escape of rustic-tinged rooms and splendid views of the lake and mountains. There are tennis courts, a pool and an excellent restaurant (see p129). ◈ *Via Silvio Bonomelli • Map E4 • 030-982-2977 • www.idue roccoli.com • €€*

7 Iseolago, Iseo
The Iseolago mixes the best of a resort hotel with the class of a fine inn, so you get parquet floors and silk drapes but also a modern fitness centre, two pools, tennis courts, and watersports at the beach. The one drawback is that it is in the suburbs, so you need a car. ◈ *Via Colombera, 2 • Map E4 • 030-98-891 • www.iseolagohotel.it • €€*

8 Villa Crespi, Lake Orta

A fantastical 1879 Moorish-style villa, complete with minaret, lies at the turn-off for Orta San Giulio. Suites and rooms are sumptuous, with either mosaic or parquet flooring, carved wooden furnishings, silk brocaded walls, and bed canopies. The restaurant serves excellent regional cuisine. ◈ *Via Fava, 18 • Map A3 • 0322-911-908 • www.lago dortahotels.com • Closed 7 Jan–13 Feb • €€€€*

9 Villa Principe Leopoldo, Lake Lugano

This bastion of 19th-century luxury overlooks Lugano from its Swiss hillside. Facilities range from a business centre to a fitness room, beauty spa and swimming pool. The Villa offers sumptuous suites; the Residence annex more subdued double rooms. ◈ *Via Montalbano 5 • Map B1 • 0041-919-858-855 • www. leopoldohotel.com • €€€€€*

10 Vittoria, Brescia
Brescia's only real hotel in the historic centre offers all the five-star amenities you could ask for in an imposing Fascist-era pile. Freestanding columns in the suites are a nice touch. Shame it's priced for businessmen's expense accounts. ◈ *Via X Giornate 20 • Map F4 • 030-280-061 • www. hotelvittoria.com • €€€€*

For hotels around the main Lakes see pp103, 113 and 123
For an explanation of price symbols see p147

Left **Camping sign** Centre **Brione camp site** Right **The pool at Campeggio Garda**

🔟 Self-Catering and Camp Sites

1 Rescasa, Milan

This is one of the main organizations for self-catering accommodation – called "Residence" in Italian, and usually available on a monthly basis. On the website is a downloadable brochure with dozens of options in Milan and throughout the region. ⊗ *Via Serbelloni 7* • *Map P2* • *02-7600-8770* • *www.rescasa.it* • *€–€€€€*

2 Santospirito Residence, Milan

A dozen classy mono-apartments right in the heart of Milan's shopping district. Expect walnut floors, satellite TVs, and flowering ivy cascading down the walls of the private courtyard. Linens are changed daily; kitchenettes cleaned twice a day. ⊗ *Via Santo Spirito 17* • *Map N2* • *02-7600-6500* • *www.santospirito.it* • *€*

3 Planet Residence, Milan

Boringly modular but spacious apartments of two or three rooms, with A/C, VCR, modem hook-ups, kitchenettes, laundry service, and thrice-weekly cleanings. Daily and weekly rates are available. ⊗ *Via Rovigno 23* • *02-2611-3753* • *www.planet residence.it* • *€€*

4 Camping Isolino, Verbania, Lake Maggiore

This oasis of tranquillity sits on the promontory of a natural reserve along a private sandy beach. It's one of the best-equipped in the region, with a market, pizzeria, restaurant, video games, pool, mountain bike excursions, Latin dancing, windsurfing lessons and even a disco. ⊗ *Via per Feriolo 25* • *Map A2* • *0323-496-080* • *www.campingisolino.com* • *Closed Oct–Mar* • *€*

5 Camping Conca d'Oro, Feriolo di Baveno, Lake Maggiore

This verdant campground lies outside Baveno in the Toce stream natural reserve. Amenities include a restaurant, mini-market, bikes and kayaks, video games and sports on a sandy beach. ⊗ *Via 42 Martiri 26* • *Map A2* • *0323 28116* • *www.concadoro.it* • *Closed Sep–Mar* • *€*

6 Camping Villaggio Gefara, Domaso, Lake Como

This small, two-star campground sits right on the beach, with a bar and laundry room, beach volleyball, and plenty of shops and watersports nearby. ⊗ *Via Case Sparse 230* • *Map C2* • *0344-96-163* • *www.campinggefara.it* • *Closed 6 Oct–27 Mar* • *€*

7 Camping Monte Brione, Riva, Lake Garda

Set in greenery near the beach, the camping and caravan site has minigolf, swimming and tennis. Small tents can be pitched amid olive terraces. ⊗ *Via Monte Brione 32* • *Map H3* • *0464-520-885* • *www.campingbrione.com* • *Closed Oct–Mar* • *€*

8 Campeggio Garda, Limone, Lake Garda

Just outside the centre of Limone, on its own private beach, this camping site offers windsurfing and sailing, and two pools, as well as a fish restaurant, wood-oven pizzeria, beach grill, and supermarket. ⊗ *Via IV Novembre 10* • *Map G3* • *0365-954-550* • *www.campinggarda.it* • *Closed Nov–Feb* • *€*

9 Camping del Sole, Lake Iseo

This large camping site offers plenty of greenery right on the lake (book ahead for the precious few lakeside sites). Facilities include a restaurant, market, cycle hire, laundry, as well as two pools and tennis and basketball courts. ⊗ *Via per Rovato* • *Map E4* • *030-980-288* • *www.campingdelsole.it* • *Closed Oct–Mar* • *€*

10 Campeggio Città di Milano

Milan's only campground is by the SS22 road to Novara (take bus 72 from the De Angeli Metro stop) near the San Siro stadium. It's got four-star facilities – pool, sports, disco – plus a waterpark nearby. ⊗ *Via G Airaghi 61* • *02-4820-0134* • *Closed 1 Dec–31 Jan* • *€*

General Index

Index

Page numbers in **bold** type refer to main entries.

A

Abbazia di Chiaravalle (abbey), Milan 92, 95
Abbazia di Piona, Lake Como 109
accommodation tips 143
  see also hotels
Agnello d'Oro hotel, Bergamo 148
agriturismi (farm stays) 143
Aimo e Nadia restaurant, Milan 68, 97
air travel 132
Alberti, Leon Battista 29, 39
Alessi kitchenware shop 78, 125
Aliseo hotel, Milan 147
Amati 35, 53
Anaunian martyrs 86
Antica Agnello restaurant, Lake Orta 129
Antica Locanda dei Mercanti hotel, Milan 144
Antica Locanda Solferino hotel, Milan 146
Antica Osteria del Vino Buono (restaurant), Bergamo 127, 129
antiques 57, 58
archaeology 16, 17
Arcimboldo, Giuseppe 17, 49
architectural styles 49
Arco della Pace, Milan 88
 Arioso Hotel, Milan 144
Ariston hotel, Milan 146
Armani 59
  clothes shop 77
  factory store 128
Arona, Lake Maggiore 99
art
  artistic styles 49
  artists 48–9
  see also decorative art, frescoes, sculpture, stone carving, and under individual artists and institutions
Ascona, Lake Maggiore 101
Asso di Fiori restaurant, Milan 97
Auditorium di Milano 60

B

Bambaia 19
banking 136
Banque, La, café and nightclub, Milan 80, 81
Bar Jamaica, Milan 90
Bar Magenta, Milan 8, 20, 65, 90, 95
Bar Margherita, Milan 90
Bar Radetzky, Milan 90
Barbarossa (Frederick I) 32
Barchetta restaurant, Bellagio 68, 69, 112
Bardolino, Lake Garda 120
Basilica di Sant'Andrea, Mantova 29, 39
Basilica di Santa Maria Maggiore, Bergamo 26
Basilica di Sant'Abbondio, Como 107
beggars 138
Bella Napoli restaurant, Riva 122
Bellagio, Lake Como 42, 43, 109, 110
Bellano, Lake Como 110
Bellini, Giovanni 12, 14, 17
Bergamo 7, 26–7, 126, 127
  Capella Colleoni 39
  Castello 27
  Galleria dell'Accademia Carrara 41
  Senterione 27
  Via Colleoni 27
Bergognone, Il 20, 24, 25, 48
Berlusconi, Silvio 33
Bernardino, Luini 48
Bialetti houseware 125
Biffi clothes shop, Milan 96
Birreria La Fontanella (bar), Milan 96
Birreria Spaten restaurant, Riva 122
boat tours see cruises
Boccioni, Umberto 12, 48, 49
Boccon di Vino restaurant, Verbania-Suna 102
Boeucc restaurant, Milan 81
Boggi clothes shop, Milan 89
books 50–51
Bormio 47
Borromeo family 46, 22–3, 99, 100
  Cardinal Frederico 73
  Carlo 98
  St Charles 33
Borromeo Palace, Isola Bella 22–3, 44, 101
Borromeo Villa, Isola Madre 101
Botticelli 18
Boulevard Café club, Milan 61, 90

Bramante 48, 73, 85
Bramantino 17
Brek restaurant, Milan 91
Brellin, El, restaurant and club, Milan 96
Brescia 126, 127
  Museo della Città 126
  Santa Giulia – Museo della Città 41
Bril 19
Broletto hotel, Mantova 148
Brunate Funicular, Como 107
budget travel 135, 140
buses 133

C

Ca' Grande, Milan 36, 76
Café Lago, Isola Bella 22
cafés and wine bars 34, 64–5
Caffè dei Funiculare, Bergamo 26
Caffè del Tasso, Bergamo 64, 65, 128
Caffè Letterario, Milan 65
Caffè Martini, Milan 80
Caffè Miró, Mantova 28
Caffè Rossi, Bellagio 106, 109
Campeggio Città di Milano camp site, Milan 149
Campeggio Garda camp site, Limone, Lake Garda 149
camping 143, 149
  see also under individual entries
Camping Conca d'Oro, Feriolo di Baveno, Lake Maggiore 149
Camping del Sole, Lake Iseo 149
Camping Isolino, Verbania, Lake Maggiore 149
Camping Monte Brione, Riva, Lake Garda 149
Camping Villaggio Gefara, Domaso, Lake Como 149
Campione d'Italia, Lake Lugano 125
Canaletto 13
Cannero Riviera, Lake Maggiore 100
Cannobio, Lake Maggiore 100
Cantinone, Il, restaurant, Milan 81
Capella Colleoni, Bergamo 26, 38, 39
Capitol hotel, Milan 145
Capo di Ponte 47
Caravaggio 13, 15, 19, 48, 49
caravanning 143
Carlton Hotel Baglioni, Milan 144

carnival (Milan) 52
car travel 132
    leasing 135
    rental 133, 141
    in Milan 139
    safety 138
carving see stone carving
Casa degli Omenoni,
    Milan 36, 37, 75, 76
Casa del Manzoni, Milan 76
Casa del Mantegna, Mantova 29
Castello di Arco,
    Lake Garda 116, 119
Castello Sforzesco, Milan 6,
    16–17, 40, 63, 85, 87
Castiglione Olona 47
castles 63
    see also under individual
        entries
Cavallino restaurant,
    Desenzano 122
Certosa di Garegnano,
    Milan 87
Certosa di Pavia 7, **24–5**, 38, 39
Chiavenna 47
children 141
churches **38–9**
    Duomo, Milan **10–11**, 38
    see also under individual
        entries
Cimitero Monumentale,
    Milan 87
Città del Sole toy shop,
    Milan 79
Civate, Lake Annone 47, 110
Civico Museo Archeologico,
    Milan 17, 40, 85
Civico Museo d'Arte
    Contemporanea, Milan 41
climbing 111, 121
clothes
    what to take 134
    see also fashion, shopping
coach travel 133
Commercio hotel, Milan 147
communications 136
Como, Lake 34, 35, **106–13**
    A Month by the Lake 50
    Bellagio 42
    Como town 39, 110
    Duomo 39, 42, 110
    itinerary 107
    lakeside towns 110
    map 106
    places to eat 112
    places to stay 113
    silk 109
    things to do 111
    Varenna 43
    Villa Balbianello 45, 50, 51
    Villa Carlotta 43, 44
    Villa Cipressi 45

Como (cont.)
    Villa Metzi 44
    Villa Monastero 45
    Villa Serbelloni 44
Conca Azzurra hotel, Ranco 103
Conservatorio Giuseppe Verdi,
    Milan 80
Corso Buenos Aires, Milan 57
Corso Como 10 café and
    clothes shop, Milan 65, 89
Corso Vittorio Emanuele II,
    Milan 56
Cotti wine and food shop,
    Milan 80
Cova café, Milan 64, 75, 80
Cracco-Peck restaurant,
    Milan 68, 81
crafts 137
Cravatterie Nazionali tie shop,
    Milan 79
credit cards 136
Crema 46
Cremona 127
    music 35, 53
Crotto dei Platani restaurant,
    Brienno 112
cruises
    Lake Como 35
    Mincio River, Mantova 29
    Navigli canal 95
    see also lakes
currency 136
customs 134, 137
cycling 53, 63, 111, 121
    Mantova 28, 62
    see also sports

D
Da Abele restaurant, Milan 91
Da Candida restaurant,
    Campione d'Italia,
    Lake Lugano 124, 129
da Vinci, Leonardo see
    Leonardo da Vinci
d'Annunzio, Gabriele 43, 45,
    118, 119
decorative art 16
Dehor nightclub, Desenzano
    121
Desenzano, Lake Garda
    119, 120
di Pietro, Antonio 33
Diana Majestic hotel,
    Milan 144
disabled travellers 140
Disco Bar Café Latino, Riva 121
Divina Commedia pub,
    Bellagio 111
diving 121
    see also sports
Dmagazine clothes shop,
    Milan 79

Dolce e Gabbana clothes shop,
    Milan 78, 89
Doll Museum,
    Rocca di Angera 99
Don Lisander restaurant 81
Doriagrand Hotel, Milan 145
Drug Store clothes shop, Il,
    Milan 89
Du Lac hotel, Bellagio 113
Due Corti, Le, hotel, Como 113
Due Roccoli, I, hotel and
    restaurant, Iseo 69, 127, 129,
    148
Due Stelle restaurant,
    Brescia 127, 129
Duomo, Como 39, 42, 107
Duomo, Mantova 28
Duomo, Milan 6, **10–11**, 34,
    62, 73
    see also Milan

E
eating out 142
    etiquette 142
    tipping 142
    understanding the menu 142
eco-tourism
    Ariston hotel, Milan 146
elderly travellers 140
electricity 134
emergencies 138
Emporio Isola clothes shop,
    Milan 89
entertainment (Milan) **60–61**
Ermenegildo Zegna 59
    clothes shop, Milan 56, 77
Esplanade restaurant,
    Desenzano 122
Etro clothes shop, Milan 78
Excelsior Hotel Gallia,
    Milan 145

F
Fabriano, Gentile da
    (artist) 12, 14
family holidays 141
fashion 52, 137
    see also clothes, shopping
Ferragamo shoe store,
    Milan 78
Ferragosto 52
Ferrè 59
    clothes shop, Milan 77
ferries 133
Festa dei Navigli, Milan 52
festivals **52–3**
films 50–51
flights see air travel
Floretta Coen Misul clothes
    shop, Milan 96
flying see air travel 132
Foix, Gaston de 16, 17

food **66–7**
 low-budget 135
 see also eating out,
 restaurants
football 53, 62
 see also sports
Forum Museum, Omegna 125
Four Seasons Hotel, Milan 144
Francesca, Piero della 13
Franco Maria Ricci books,
 Milan 79
Francis I 17
Frederick I Barbarossa 32
frescoes
 Leonardo's *Last Supper* 6,
 8–9, 38, 85
 see also churches
Frette clothes shop, Milan 78
Fura Club, Lonato 121

G
Galleria d'Arte Moderna e
 Contemporanea, Bergamo 27
Galleria dell'Accademia Carrara,
 Bergamo 27, 41
Galleria Taldini, Lovere 126
Galleria Vittorio Emanuele II
 shopping arcade, Milan 10,
 36, 56, 72, 74, 75
galleries
 Pinacoteca di Brera,
 Milan 6, **12–15**
 see also under individual
 entries
Garda, Lake 35, **116–23**
 and D H Lawrence 50
 Gardaland theme park 62,
 63, 117, 139
 Gardone Riviera 119, 120
 Giardino Botanico Hruska
 43, 45
 itinerary 119
 lakeside towns 120
 map 116
 places to eat 122
 places to stay 123
 Sirmione 43
 things to do 121
 Vittoriale, Il 43, 45
 windsurfing 63
Gardaland theme park
 62, 63, 117, 139
gardens
 Giardino Botanico Hruska,
 Lake Garda 43
 see also villas and gardens,
 and Isole Borromee
Gardesana restaurant,
 Torri del Benaco 122
Gardone Riviera, Lake Garda
 119, 120
Garibaldi, General 33

Gastronomia Peck
 delicatessen, Milan 18, 79
gay and lesbian travellers 140
Gemma restaurant, Limone 122
Genius Hotel Downtown,
 Milan 146
getting around Milan
 and the Lakes 133
 see also travel
Gianfranco Ferré 59
 clothes shop, Milan 77
Gianni Versace 59
 clothes shop, Milan 77
Giardino Botanico Hruska,
 Gardone Riviera 43, 45, 116,
 118, 119, 120
Giorgio Armani 59
 clothes shop, Milan 77
Giotto (artist) 14
Girasole, Il restaurant,
 Sirmione 122
Giulio Cesare hotel, Milan 146
golf 53, 121, 111
 see also sports
Gonzaga family 28, 29
 Duke Vespasiano 127
Grand Café Fashion café and
 nightclub, Milan 96
Grand Hotel de Milan 144
Grand Hôtel et des Iles
 Borromées, Stresa 103
Grand Hotel Fieramilano,
 Milan 145
Grand Hotel, Locarno 103
Grand Hotel, Menaggio 113
Grand Hotel Majestic,
 Verbania-Pallanza 103
Grand Hotel restaurant,
 Milan 97
Grand Hotel, Tremezzo 113
Grand Hotel Villa Serbelloni,
 Bellagio 108, 113
Grand Prix, Monza 52, 53
Gran Duca di York hotel,
 Milan 146
Gravedona, Lake Como 110
Grifone hotel, Sirmione 123
Gritti hotel, Milan 147
Grotte di Catullo,
 Sirmione 117, 119
Gucci clothes shop,
 Milan 78

H
H V Morton 51, 73
haggling 137
Hayez, Francesco
 (artist) 13, 15, 49
health 138
 food and water 138
Hemingway pub,
 Como 111

Hemingway, Ernest 50
hiking 35, 53
history **32–3**, 119
Hollywood nightclub,
 Milan 61, 90
horse racing 53
horse riding 53, 111
 see also sports
hospitals 138
Hostaria Borromei restaurant,
 Milan 81
hostels 143
Hotel de la Ville, Milan 144
Hotel du Lac et du Park,
 Riva del Garda 123
Hotel Executive,
 Milan 145
Hotel Impero, Cremona 148
hotels 103, 143
 booking 139
 budget 135, 147
 business (Milan) 145
 luxury (Milan) 144
 mid-range (Milan) 146
 outside Milan 148
 see also entries for individual
 hotels and pensiones
Hotel Sempione, Milan 147
Hotel Star, Milan 146

I
ice-cream parlours *(gelaterie)* 62
Ice Nice café, Milan 80
immigration 134
information 134
internet access 136
Intra, Lake Maggiore 100
Ippodromo, Milan 53, 88
Iseo, Lake Iseo 126
Iseolago hotel, Iseo 148
Isola Bella 101
 Borromeo Palace **22–3**
 grottoes 22
 see also Isole Borromee
Isola di Garda, Lake Garda 118
Isola Madre 98, 101
 Borromeo Villa 23
 botanical gardens 23
 see also Isole Borromee
Isola dei Pescatori (Isola
 Superiore) 101
Isola San Giulio 125
Isola Superiore (dei Pescatori)
 101
Isole Borromee, Lake Maggiore
 7, **22–3**, 42, 100, 101
Italian State Tourism Board 134

J
Jacopo Bassano 19
Jesi, Maria 14
Joia restaurant, Milan 68, 91

K

kayaking 111
see also sports
Kennedy *pensione*, Milan 147
Krizia 59
clothes shop, Milan 77
Kursaal nightclub, Sirmione 121

L

lakes
Annone 47
Biandronno 125
camping 149
Comábbio 125
cruises 35, 109
ferries 109, 110
golf 53
hiking 53
hill walking 35
Idro 126
in winter 139
Iseo 47, 126, 127
lakeside attractions **42–3**
Lugano 125
Orta 125
Monate 125
sailing 53
shopping **56–9**
skiing 53
surfing 35
Varese 125
villas and gardens **44–5**
windsurfing 53
see also Como, Garda,
Maggiore, smaller lakes
and towns
Last Supper 6, **8–9**, 38,
85
booking 139
see also Leonardo da Vinci
Latteria San Marco café,
Milan 87, 91
Laura Biagiotti clothes shop,
Milan 78
Lecco, Lake Como 110
Lenno, Lake Como 110
Leonardo da Vinci **8–9**, 14, 16,
18, 38, 48, 62, 93
Codex Atlantico 18, 40
Museo Nazionale della
Scienza e della Tecnica –
Leonardo da Vinci, Milan 40
Last Supper 6, **8–9**, 38, 85
Leoncino Rosso restaurant,
Mantova 124, 129
Leoni, Leone 76
Libreria Internazionale Accademia
book store, Milan 79
Lido Giardino, Menaggio 111
Limelight club, Milan 60, 96
Limone sul Garda,
Lake Garda 119, 120

Linate airport
see also air travel 132
Locanda dell'Isola Comacina
restaurant, Ossuccio 109, 112
Locarno, Lake Maggiore 101
Lodi 46
Logostina housewares shop,
Crusinallo-Omegna,
Lake Orta 128
Lombard experiences **34–5**
Lombard League 33
London hotel, Milan 146
Lorenzetti, Ambrogio 14
Lotto, Lorenzo 41
Lovere 126
Lubiam clothes shop,
Mantova 128
Luini 19
Luini food bar, Milan 81

M

Maderno *see*
Toscolano–Maderno
Magazzini Generali club,
Milan 61
Maggiore, Lake 42, **98–103**
Borromeo Palace **22–3**, 44
Isole Borromee **22–3**
itinerary 101
map 98
places to eat 102
places to stay 103
Rocca di Anghera 42
Santa Caterina del Sasso
church 42
Stresa 50
Villa Taranto 44
Malcesine hotel,
Malcesine 123
Malcesine, Lake Garda 120
Malpensa airport
see also air travel 132
Mantegna, Andrea 12, 14, 16,
17, 28, 29, 48
Mantova 7, **28–9**, 124, 126, 127
Basilica di Sant'Andrea 39
cycling 63
Manzoni hotel, Milan 146
Manzoni, Alessandro
50, 106, 110
Marconi, Giuglielmo 93
Mario Buccellati jewellery
shop, Milan 78
Marriott hotel, Milan 145
Max Mara clothes shop,
Milan 78
Mazzarditi brothers 100
medical costs 138
Mediolanum hotel, Milan 145
Melide, Lake Lugano 125
Memphis design shop,
Milan 89

Menaggio, Lake Como 110
menus 142
see also eating out
Mezzegra, Lake Como 110
Mialno restaurant,
Verbania-Pallanza 102
Michelangelo 16
Mila Schön 59
clothes shop, Milan 77
Milan **6–7**, **36–7**, **72–81**, **84–91**,
92–7
cafés 34
camping 149
cathedral (Duomo) **10–11**, 73
driving 139
entertainment **60–61**
football 53
horse racing 53
hotel booking 139
in August 139
markets 57
metro 133
Museo del Duomo 11
Navigli district 34, 35, 92,
93, 95
opera 35, 41
Parco Sempione 17
Pinacoteca di Brera 6, **12–15**
Sant'Ambrogio church **20–21**
Scala, La 35
shopping 34, **56–9**
see also churches, Milan's
historic centre, museums,
northern Milan, southern
Milan
Milan's historic centre **72–81**
best of the rest 76
fashion shops 77
itinerary 75
map 72
other designer shops 78
other high-class shops 79
places to eat 81
venues, clubs and cafés 80
see also Milan
Milanese restaurant, La,
Milan 68, 81
Milano *pensione*, Varenna 113
Missoni 59
clothes shop, Milan 77
Modamilano 52
Modigliani 15
monasteries
Certosa di Pavia 7, **24–5**
money 135
Montarrone 101
Monte Verità, Lake Maggiore
101
Monza
Grand Prix 52, 53
Mortarotti clothes shop,
Milan 79

Index

Moschino 59
  clothes shop, Milan 77
motor racing 52, 53
Murrina, La, Milan 79
Musei Civici, Varese 125
Museo Archeologico,
  Milan 17, 40, 41, 85
Museo Bagatti Valsecchi,
  Milan 75
Museo del Cinema, Milan 37
Museo del Duomo, Milan 73
Museo del Giocattolo,
  Milan 62
Museo della Città,
  Brescia 126
Museo della Storia Naturale,
  Milan 87, 88
Museo dell'Ottocento,
  Milan 84, 87
Museo del Risorgimento,
  Milan 88
Museo di Milano 76
Museo Diocesano,
  Milan 20, 93, 95
Museo Donizettiano,
  Bergamo 27
Museo Nazionale della Scienza
  e della Tecnica – Leonardo da
  Vinci, Milan 40, 62, 93, 95
Museo Poldi-Pezzoli, Milan 40,
  74, 75
Museo Stradivariano,
  Cremona 127
Museo Teatrale alla Scala,
  Milan 41, 88
Museum of Silk, Como 108
museums **40–41**, 87
  also under individual entries
music
  concerts 60–61, 80
  Cremona 35, 53, 127, 128
  festivals 99, 101
  see also opera
musical instruments 16
Mussolini, Benito 32, 33, 43,
  110, 120, 123

N
Nadro di Ceto 47
Napoleon Bonaparte 10, 12, 13
Navigli district, Milan 34, 35,
  92, 93, 95, 97
Nepentha nightclub, Milan 80
newspapers 134
Nicolin restaurant, Lecco 112
Northern League 33
Northern Milan **84–91**
  best of the rest 88
  cafés and entertainment
    venues 90
  itinerary 87
  map 84

Northern Milan (cont.)
  places to eat 91
  shops 89
Notte, La 51
Nuovo hotel, Milan 147

O
Oblò pub, Mantova 128
Ochina Bianca restaurant,
  Mantova 129
Oh bej! Oh bej!, Milan 53
Omegna 125
opera 35, 51, 53
  Cremona 128
  Museo Teatrale alla Scala,
    Milan 41
Ostello La Primula hostel and
  restaurant, Menaggio 112
Ostello Piero Rotta hostel,
  Milan 147
Osteria degli Amici, Stresa 102

P
Paganini hotel, Milan 147
palaces see under individual
  entries
palazzi of Via Manzoni, Milan 76
Palazzo d'Arco, Mantova 29
Palazzo della Ragione,
  Milan 36, 73, 75
Palazzo di Brera 13
Palazzo Ducale, Mantova 28
Palazzo Dugnani,
  Milan 37, 87, 88
Palazzo Litta, Milan 36, 88
Palazzo Marino,
  Milan 36, 37, 75, 76
Palazzo Reale, Milan 73
Palazzo Te, Mantova 29
Pallanza, Lake Maggiore 100
Palma hotel, La, Stresa 103
Palme hotel, Le,
  Limone sul Garda 123
Panini della Befi, I, café,
  Milan 80
Papageno Pub, Bergamo 128
paragliding 121
Parco Sempione, Milan 17, 85
Park Hotel Villa Cortine 123
Park Hotel, Desenzano 123
Park Hyatt Milan hotel,
  Milan 144
Pasticceria Marchesi,
  Milan 65, 90, 95
Pavia 46
  Certosa di Pavia 7, **24–5**
Peck, Milan (bar and food
  emporium) 18, 79
Perugino 24
pharmacies 138
Piazza del Comune,
  Cremona 124, 126
Piazza del Duomo, Como 106

pickpockets 138, 139
Piemontese restaurant,
  Stresa 102
Pinacoteca Ambrosiana,
  Milan 7, **18–19**, 40, 73, 75
Pinacoteca di Brera,
  Milan 6, **12–15**, 40, 86
Pirelli Tower, Milan 37, 88
Pironi hotel, Cannobio 103
Pizzeria Grand'Italia, Milan 91
Pizzeria Vecchia Napoli,
  Milan 91
Planet Residence, Milan 149
Plastic nightclub, Milan 61
Pliny 107, 108
police 138
Pont de Ferr, Al, restaurant,
  Milan 68, 97
Ponte Rosso restaurant,
  Milan 97
Porta Nuova, Milan 88
Portici del Comune, I, café,
  Cremona 64, 65, 128
Portico, Il, hotel, Cannobio 103
postal service 136
Prada 59
  clothes shop, Milan 77
prehistory 35
rock carvings 35
Premiata Pizzeria, Milan 97
Primavera hotel, Stresa 103
Principe de Savoia hotel,
  Milan 144
Promessi Sposi, I 50
  see also Manzoni,
    Alessandro
puppet shows 62

Q
Quadrilatero d'Oro shopping
  area 57, 72, 75

R
Raccolta dei Violini, Cremona
  127
Raphael 13, 15, 19, 40
Rescasa (self-catering holidays)
  149
restaurants **68–9**, 142
Ricordi music store, Milan 79
Ristorante Anzani, Milan 91
Ristorante del Pescatore,
  Stresa 102
Ristorante Sociale, Como 112
Riva del Garda,
  Lake Garda 119, 120
  sports 121
Rocca di Angera,
  Lake Maggiore 42, 98, 99
Rocca Scaligera,
  Lake Garda 117, 119
rock carvings 35

Rockefeller Foundation 108
Rolling Stone nightclub,
    Milan 60, 61, 96
Romano, Giulio 28, 29, 49
Romantik Hotel Laurin,
    Salò 123
Rotonda di Via Besana church,
    Milan 92, 93
Rotonda di San Lorenzo,
    Mantova 29
Rovello hotel, Milan 146
Rucola, La, restaurant,
    Sirmione 122
Rufus shoe shop, Milan 89

S

Sabbioneta 46, 127
Sadler restaurant, Milan 97
safety 138
    valuables 139
Sagra del Carroccio, Legnano 52
sailing 53
St Ambrose 21, 33, 86
St Augustine 33
St Charles Borromeo 33
Salò, Lake Garda 120
Salvagente, Il, clothes shop,
    Milan 96
San Fedele church, Milan 74, 75
San Gottardo chapel, Milan 76
San Lorenzo hotel,
    Bergamo 148
San Lorenzo hotel,
    Mantova 148
San Lorenzo Maggiore church,
    Milan 38, 92, 93, 95
San Marco church,
    Milan 86, 87
San Nazaro Maggiore church,
    Milan 76
San Sempliciano church,
    Milan 86, 87
San Sepolcro church, Milan 76
San Siro (Stadio Meazza),
    Milan 88
Santa Caterina del Sasso
    church, Lake Maggiore 42,
    98, 99
Santa Giulia – Museo della
    Città, Brescia 41
Santa Maria church presso
    San Celso, Milan 93
Santa Maria church presso
    San Satiro, Milan 38, 73, 75
Santa Maria della Neve church,
    Pisogne 126
Santa Maria della Passione
    church, Milan 93
Santa Maria delle Grazie
    church, Milan 8, 38, 85
Santa Marta hotel,
    Milan 146

Sant'Ambrogio church,
    Milan 7, **20–21**, 38, 93
Sant'Ambroseus café,
    Milan 64, 80
Sant'Eustorgio church,
    Milan 38, 39, 93, 95
Santospirito Residence,
    Milan 149
Scala, La, opera house, Milan
    35, 51, 53, 60, 74, 80
    museum 41, 88
    see also opera
Scalo, Lo, restaurant,
    Cannobio 102
Scarlet club, Como 111
Scimmie restaurant and club,
    Milan 60, 96
sculpture
    in Il Duomo, Milan 10–11
    see also stone carving,
        Castello Sforzesco, Certosa
        di Pavia, churches
self-catering holidays 149
    Rescasa 149
Sesto Senso Club,
    Desenzano 121
Sette Porte, Le, restaurant,
    Como 112
settimane musicali, Stresa 52
Sforza, Francesco 16, 32, 36
    see also Castello Sforzesco,
        Milan
Sforza, Galeazzo Maria 32, 33
Sforza, Lodovico "Il Moro"
    33, 47
shopping 34
    opening hours 134, 137
    prices 139
    shipping home 137
    tax refunds 137
    tips 135, 137
Sigurtà Gardens, Lake Garda 117
Silbemagl home-furnishing
    store, Milan 79
Sirmione, Lake Garda
    42, 43, 119, 120
smaller lakes and towns **124–9**
    itinerary 127
    map 124
    places to eat 129
    shops, cafés and nightspots
        128
Sole, Il, hotel and restaurant,
    Ranco 69, 102, 103
Sole hotel, Riva del Garda 123
Sosta, La, restaurant,
    Cremona 129
Southern Milan **92–7**
    itinerary 95
    map 92
    places to eat 97
    shops and nightspots 96

Specchio di Alice second-hand
    clothes, Milan 96
Spadari al Duomo hotel,
    Milan 144
Sperlari sweet shop,
    Cremona 128
Speronari hotel, Milan 147
sports 53
    Lake Garda 121
    Lake Idro 126
    see also under individual
        sports
Stadio Meazza see San Siro
Stazione Centrale, Milan 37
stone carving
    in Il Duomo, Milan **10–11**
    in Certosa di Pavia **24–5**
    in Sant'Ambrogio, Milan **20–21**
    see also churches
Stradivari, Antonio
    33, 35, 53, 127
    Museo Stradivariano 127
Stresa, Lake Maggiore
    50, 98, 99, 101
    settimane musicale 52
student travellers 140
Suisse hotel, Bellagio 113
Sukrity restaurant, Milan 91
Suna, Lake Maggiore 100
surfing (windsurfing)
    Lake Garda 35
Surplus clothing store,
    Milan 89
Swiss Miniatur 125

T

Taverna del Colleoni & del
    Angelo, Bergamo 129
taxis 133
Teatro all'Antica, Sabbioneta 127
Teatro degli Arcimboldi,
    Milan 90
Teatro del Four Seasons, Il,
    restaurant, Milan 68, 81
Teatro delle Marionette,
    Milan 62
Teatro Donizetti, Bergamo 27
Teatro Ponchielli, Cremona 128
Teatro Scientifico Bibiena,
    Mantova 29
telephones 136
television 134
Terrazza, La, restaurant,
    Milan 87, 91
theatres
    Teatro all'Antica,
        Sabbioneta 127
    Teatro degli Arcimboldi,
        Milan 90
    Teatro Donizetti, Bergamo 27
    Teatro Scientifico Bibiena,
        Mantova 29

Index

theatres (cont.)
  see also opera
theme parks
  Gardaland, Lake Garda 63, 117
Theodolinda 33
Tintoretto 13, 14
Tipica Osteria Pugliese
  restaurant, Milan 91
tipping 142
Titian 14, 19
Tombon de San Marc, El,
  bar, Milan 90
Torbole, Lake Garda 120
  see also sports
Torre Velasca, Milan 36, 76
Torri del Benaco,
  Lake Garda 116, 118
Toscanini, Arturo 51, 74
Toscolano–Maderno,
  Lake Garda 120
tourist information 134
train travel 132, 133
  discounts 135, 141
trams 133
Trattoria Aurora, Milan 97
Trattoria Campagna,
  Arona 102
Trattoria da Pino, Milan 81
Trattoria Famiglia Conconi
  restaurant, Milan 97
Trattoria S Stefano, Lenno 112
travel
  public holidays 134
  when to go 134, 135
  see also air travel, train
  travel, tourist information
travellers' cheques 136
Tremezzo, Lake Como 106, 110
Trussardi 59
  clothes shop, Milan 77
Tunnel nightclub, Milan 61, 90

U
Una Hotel Century, Milan 145
Una Hotel Cusani, Milan 145

V
Val Calmonica 47, 127
Valentino clothes shop,
  Milan 78
Valtellina 47
Varenna, Lake Como
  43, 109, 110
Vecchia Arona, La, restaurant,
  Arona 102
Vecchia Malcesine restaurant,
  Malcesine 122
Vecchia Menaggio restaurant,
  Menaggio 112
Vecchia Milano hotel,
  Milan 147
Vecchia Varenna restaurant,
  Varenna 109, 112
Verbania, Lake Maggiore 100
Verbano hotel and restaurant,
  Isola Superiore 101, 102, 103
Veronese, Paolo 14
Versace 59
  clothes shop 77
Vestimoda Stock
  discount shop, Milan 89
Via Borgospesso, Milan 57
Via della Spiga, Milan 57
Via Manzoni, Milan 56
  palazzi 76
Via Montenapoleone,
  Milan 56, 57, 59, 75
Via P Verri, Milan 56
Via San Gregorio,
  Milan 57
Vigevano 46, 47
Vigne, Le, restaurant,
  Milan 97
Villa Balbianello, Lake Como
  45, 50, 51, 107
Villa Belgiojoso Bonaparte,
  Milan 86, 87
Villa Carlotta, Lake Como 43,
  44, 108, 109
Villa Cipressi hotel,
  Lake Como 45, 109, 113

Villa Crespi hotel and
  restaurant,
  Lake Orta 129, 148
Villa d'Este hotel,
  Cernobbio 113
Villa Fiordaliso hotel and
  restaurant, Gardone Riviera
  69, 119, 122, 123
Villa Flori hotel, Como 113
villa holidays 143
Villa Melzi, Bellagio 44, 106,
  108
Villa Monastero, Lake Como
  44, 45, 108, 109
Villa Principe Leopoldo hotel,
  Lake Lugano 148
Villa Romana, Desenzano 118,
  119, 120
Villa Serbelloni, Bellagio 44, 108
Villa Taranto,
  Lake Maggiore 44, 100
villas and gardens 22–3, **44–5**
Vineria Cozzi wine bar,
  Bergamo 65, 128
Visconti, Gian Galeazzo 24, 25,
  33, 39
Visconti, Ottone 32
Vittoria hotel, Brescia 148
Vittoriale, Il, Gardone Riviera
  43, 45, 116, 118, 119, 120
Volta, Alessandro 33

W
water 138
Westin Palace hotel,
  Milan 145
windsurfing 53, 63, 111, 121
wine bars **64–5**
wine 59, 67, 137, 142
  Bardolino 120
women travellers 140

Z
Zucca café (Caffè Miani),
  Milan 10, 56, 64, 75, 80

Acknowledgements

The Author
Reid Bramblett is a travel writer who currently lives in New York. He has written guides to Italy, Europe and New York for Frommer's and is the author of DK's *Top 10 Tuscany*.

Produced by
BLUE ISLAND PUBLISHING,
London
www.blueisland.co.uk

Editorial Director
Rosalyn Thiro

Art Director
Stephen Bere

Associate Editor
Michael Ellis

Editors
Charlotte Rundall, Jane Simmonds

Designer
Lee Redmond

Picture Research
Ellen Root

Research Assistance
Amaia Allende

Proofreader
Jane Simmonds

Fact-checker
Sylvia Gallotti

Indexer
Charlotte Rundall

Main Photographers
Paul Harris and Anne Heslope

Additional Photography
Steve Bere, John Heseltine, Clive Streeter.

Cartography
James Anderson, Jane Voss (Anderson Geographics Ltd)

AT DORLING KINDERSLEY

Publisher
Douglas Amrine

Publishing Manager
Anna Streiffert

Senior Art Editor
Marisa Renzullo

Senior Cartographic Editor
Casper Morris

Senior DTP Designer
Jason Little

Production
Melanie Dowland

Additional Editorial Assistance
Sally-Ann Bloomfield, Michelle Crane, Sands Publishing Solutions, Ellie Smith

Photography Permissions
Dorling Kindersley would like to thank all the cathedrals, churches, museums, hotels, restaurants, bars, clubs, shops, galleries and other sights for their assistance and kind permission to photograph.

Placement Key: t = top; tl = top left; tr = top right; tc = top centre; c= centre; cr = centre right; b= bottom; bl = bottom left; br = bottom right.

Acknowledgements

Works of art have been reproduced with the permission of the following copyright holders:

ARCHIVIO ISTITUTO GEOGRAFICO DEAGOSTINI: 24br, 24bl; ARCHIVO STORICO DEL CINEMA/ AFE: directed by Mario Camerini 50tl, directed by Michelangelo Antonioni 50tr, directed by Charles Vidor 50c, directed by Vittorio De Sica 50b.

BRIDGEMAN ART LIBRARY, London: Biblioteca Ambrosiana, Milan 48tc; Ognissanti, Florence Sabdro Botticelli Detail from *St Augustine in his Study* 33tr; Museo del Duomo Tintoretto *Christ Among the Doctors* 73b; Pinacoteca Ambrosiana 7tl, 18c, 18-19; Pinacoteca di Brera 13c, 14cl, 15b, 48b; Sandro Boticelli *Portrait of Guiliano de' Medici* 27b; Private Collection 32tr, 33cr.

CORBIS: Ted Spiegel 46tr; Sandro Vannini 47t.

FMR spa: 79r

GENIUS RESORT: 146tr.

MAGAZZINI GENERALI: 61t; FOTO MAJRANI, MILANO: supplied by Ikona 25t; MARKA: 40tr; M Albonico 85t, 87br; T Conti 6bl, 12c, 14t, 40tl, 52tr; M Cristofori 40b; C Dogliani 40tc; D Donadoni 7tr, 24-5 27t, 60b; G Ferrari 52c; F Garufi 33br; S Malli 8t, 24t, 53bl, 88tr; G Mereghetti 52tl; Foto OM 53tr; F Pizzochero 66tr, 67tl. RISTORANTE CAVALLINO: 122tl; ROLLING STONE: 60tr; ROVELLO HOTEL:146tl.

SANTA MARTA HOTEL: 146tc; © PHOTO SCALA, Florence: Biblioteca Marucelliana, Firenze Leoni Ottavio 48tr; Biblioteca Reale, Torino 48c; Castello Sforenzesco 16t, 16b, 16-17, 17t, 17b; Galleria degli Uffizi - courtesy of the Ministero Beni e Att. Culturali 32bl; Museo Poldi-Pezzoli 41b, 75b; Museo Teatrale alla Scala © DACS 2005 41t; Palazzo Ducale Venezia Federico Zuccari *Il Barbarossa bacia il piede a papa Alessandro III* 32tl; Pinacoteca Ambrosiana 18b, 19c, 19b; Pinacoteca di Brera 12t, 12b, 12-13, 13b, 14b, 15t, 48tl; Sant'Ambrogio 20t, 20bl, 20br, 21t, 21c, 20-21, 21b; Santa Maria delle Grazie 6tl, 8c(d), 8b(d), 9t(d), 8-9, 9b(d), 30-1.

UFFICIO STAMPA ORCHETRA VERDI: Silvia Lelli 60tl.

All other images are © Dorling Kindersley. For more information see www.dkimages.com

Dorling Kindersley Special Editions

Dorling Kindersley books can be purchased in bulk quantities at discounted prices for use in promotions or as premiums. We are also able to offer special editions and personalized jackets, corporate imprints, and excerpts from all of our books, tailored specifically to meet your own needs.

To find out more, please contact: (in the United Kingdom) – Sarah.Burgess@dk.com or Special Sales, Dorling Kindersley Limited, 80 Strand, London WC2R 0RL; (in the United States) – Special Markets Department, DK Publishing, Inc., 375 Hudson Street, New York, New York 10014.